Hooking Mats and Rugs

33 New Designs
from an Old Tradition

Deanne Fitzpatrick

Creative Publishing
international

Creative Publishing international

Copyright © 2007 Nimbus Publishing
All rights reserved

First published in the United States of America in 2008 by
Creative Publishing international, a member of
Quayside Publishing Group
400 First Avenue North
Suite 300
Minneapolis, MN 55401
1-800-328-3895
www.creativepub.com

Due to differing conditions, materials, and skill levels, the publisher and various manufacturers disclaim any liability for unsatisfactory results or injury due to improper use of tools, materials, or information in this publication.

ISBN-13: 978-1-58923-380-5
ISBN-10: 1-58923-380-8

10 9 8 7 6 5 4 3 2 1

Library of Congress Cataloging-in-Publication Data
Fitzpatrick, Deanne.
  Hooking mats and rugs : 33 new designs from an old tradition / Deanne Fitzpatrick.
     p. cm.
  ISBN 1-58923-380-8
  1. Rugs, Hooked--Atlantic Provinces. 2. Pictorial rugs--Atlantic Provinces. I. Title.

  TT850.F55 2008
  746.7'4--dc22

                                    2007035078
                                         CIP

Book Design: Creative Publishing international, Inc.
Cover Design: Creative Publishing international, Inc.
Page Layout: Megan Cooney
Illustrations: Deanne Fitzpartrick
Photographs: Deanne Fitzpatrick; Megan Lewis, p. 18; Chris Reardon, p. 128

Printed in China

Cover: *Living on the Edge,* 10" x 12" (25.4 x 30.5 cm)
A portion of the vignette on pages 58–59 was printed in the Art Gallery of Nova Scotia's catalog
One for Sorrow Two for Joy, 1996.

DEDICATION

To my Uncle Donald Fitzpatrick, who first took me around the bay to
Paradise and Petite Forte and showed me where we came from. It was a trip
that transformed my father's childhood stories from magic to memory. I carry
it with me.

ACKNOWLEDGMENTS

Nothing is ever created alone. I am surrounded by love and support on all sides.
Together, my family and friends keep me afloat. Special thanks to Brenda Clarke,
who carefully looked over the projects in this book and offered suggestions. She
is a faithful friend and helps me in the studio year after year. Louitta Sears and
Cathy Carter have helped me in the studio for many years, and they make my
work and life easier. Adele Mansour tells me what I need to know and teaches me
how to be a good mother. Mikhial Mansour gives me the gift of time, time and
time again. Robert Mansour has been there from the first loop that I hooked.
Thanks to all of you. I need you all, count on you, and appreciate you.

Contents

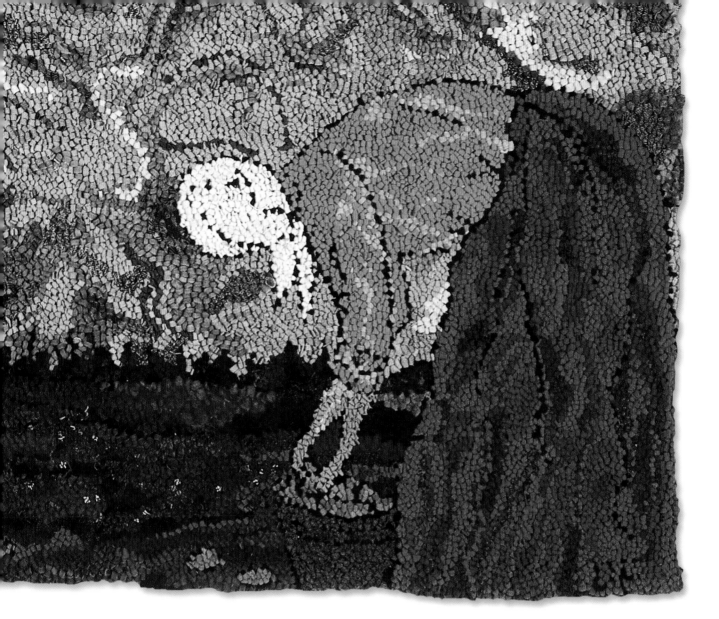

THE POTATO PICKERS
7' x 3' (2.1 x 0.9 m)

CHAPTER 1

The Story of Rug Hooking

Primitive rug hooking is believed to be a craft indigenous to North America. No doubt it has roots in the European settlers' home countries—but the unique tradition of tearing worn-out clothing into strips and then hooking it, loop by loop, onto an old burlap feed bag (with a hook that's been fashioned from a curved nail and a wooden handle) seems to have emerged somewhere along the eastern seaboard of North America in the early to mid-1800s. Of course, the strong traditions of other types of rug making and needlework in Europe, Asia, and India undoubtedly had an impact on the development of this craft in North America. Wherever it began, and however it developed, rug hooking is a craft that grew out of necessity. Early settlers battling the elements needed to warm their homes. Drafty floors were covered with rugs made out of cast-off clothing.

Rug hooking, known as mat making in Atlantic Canada, was also a pastime when the day's work was done. Both my father and mother talked about how their own mothers loved to work on hooked mats. The mats reminded my father of his mother in the kitchen by the comfort of the stove, where she kept her mat "bars" (the hooking frame). She was known for her ability to draw patterns. She would take a piece of charred wood from the fire and draw a design onto an old feed bag. Often she would draw patterns for other women in the community to hook—for example, a simple "boat with a house and a path going up to it," as my uncle once recalled. When she ran out of old clothes to hook with, she would take apart the brin (burlap) bag, dye the strands, and hook several strands together onto another feed bag.

At any given time, my grandmother Emma Wakeham Fitzpatrick would have twenty to thirty mats spread around the floors of her coral-colored flattop house. The best of these would be rolled up underneath the bed to spread in the parlor when the parish priest made his yearly visit. The next best were in the bedrooms, and the hit-and-miss rugs—made with bits of leftover scraps—were relegated to the kitchen or the back porch. As the rugs lost their shine, they migrated from the parlor, to the bedrooms, to the foot of the stairs, and into the kitchen, finally landing at the back door as they neared the end of their usefulness.

During the early twentieth century, women in Atlantic Canada sold or traded hooked rugs and mats to peddlers who went door to door and who later sold the rugs themselves. I smile at the thought of a woman with no money of her own being able to hook rugs to make a little cash or trade for a square of linoleum to decorate her kitchen.

LEAVING
40" x 30" (1 x 0.76 m)

This rug is about how difficult it is to stay and watch other people leave. So often our children grow up and move away for work, better paying jobs, or adventure. There are so many departures. Since I was a child, I have watched people going away. I count myself as one of the lucky ones, in that circumstances, and choices, have enabled me to stay in Atlantic Canada.

My aunt told me that one of her least-favorite chores was cleaning the mats. She would have to shake them out, haul them down to the wharf to dip them in salt water, ring them out, and lay them on the fish flakes to dry. No doubt this rigorous cleaning led to an early demise for many of the loveliest rugs—water is terribly hard on burlap, causing it to rot quickly. In short, hooked rugs were an everyday part of the household. They were not the valued treasures they are today.

In the early 1900s, catalogs offered women the opportunity to buy "stamped backs" or commercial patterns, and rug hooking increased in popularity. As linoleum and later commercial carpeting became more readily available, hooked rugs or mats went out of style. As a girl growing up in Newfoundland in the 1970s, I remember only one or two women hooking rugs. By then it was a pastime of a bygone era.

My mother, who had to hook on a mat every day after school to help her mother, described it as "a chore of poverty." When I first began hooking rugs, she was surprised by my interest. She was even more surprised later on when I began to sell my rugs. She would say, "Deanne, I can't believe people are giving you money for hooked mats!" It wasn't that she didn't like my rugs, it was just that in the sixty years since she had given up hooking, she had seen little or no interest in the craft. She did start to hook rugs again in her seventies, I am happy to say, and made fourteen more rugs before she died. She enjoyed it as a great pastime and preferred to make the traditional floral designs with hit-and-miss border blocks that her mother had taught her to make.

Rug hooking never entirely disappeared in North America. For years it continued on, but outside of popular culture. It has endured as a craft and is still developing as an art. There are many active guilds and makers throughout North America who ensure that rug hooking continues to thrive and grow.

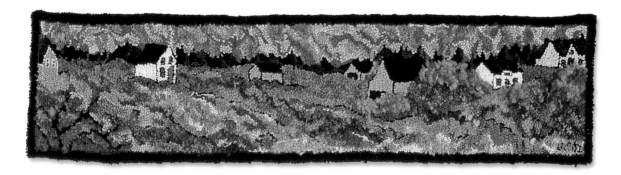

CHAPMAN SETTLEMENT ROAD

73" x 20" (1.8 x 0.5 m)

This is a road I had walked along for years, and one day in late August it looked as if it had transformed itself. The light and the season completely changed the way it looked, making it even more beautiful.

MY INSPIRATION

I grew up in a tall, three-story, white clapboard house perched on a rocky hill. It was bound at the back by tall dark spruce. It looked as if it was tilted slightly toward the sea. Although it lay on a cement foundation, the windows rattled and the house shook a little at night.

The hill below our house was scattered with a few houses, mostly in shades of white and yellow. I was the little girl kneeling against the back of a big armchair in the middle window of the second floor of the house. From this perch, I watched the waves beating against the rock, the slight changes in the tide, the color of the water, the boats coming home from the inshore fishery, and the goings-on of our little coastal community. I would watch the women going back and forth to bingo games, men in gray suits walking down the hill to attend church service, boys heading off to the pond with skates, laces tied together, slung over their shoulders. When I saw girls out and about, I usually joined them. The activities would change with the day and time of year. This period was the beginning of my life as an artist, although I had no idea of that at the time. At that window on that coast, the simplicity of life sunk into my being.

The coast that I grew up on was rugged. The water was too cold and rough to swim in. Houses were built a sensible distance from the shore, showing respect for the sea. It was not a water to fool around with. It was there for the fishery. I was taught to respect the water and to watch myself around it. It could be relied upon for a livelihood, but it could never be trusted. The only time I let my feet get wet in the waves was during capelin season, when I carried my empty salt beef bucket close to the water to fill it up with the little silver fish that were still abundant in the 1970s. The only seashells I saw were the shells of green spiky sea urchins, deep blue mussels, and the small white barnacles permanently fastened to the big dark rocks below the meadow. There were always a few old carved buoys lying about, bits of net and plastic, cork, mermaids' purses, and rope to collect and play with. Day after day, I would fill egg cartons with rocks of different colors, shades, and shapes, and with other bits to carry home. I still do this kind of thing today. Once a gatherer, always a gatherer.

I got the idea for this rug while driving to Parrsboro. The side of a steep hill was littered with people picking blueberries. Most blueberries are picked with mechanical harvesters, but in certain fields, the steepness of the slope makes that impossible. Harvesting—whether done by a bunch of people in straw hats gathering rhubarb or berries, or a lone man picking peas in the garden—always takes my breath away. It is such a beautiful, basic part of being human. We all know the goodness, the freshness of the harvest, and the importance of getting it in. Watching people gather, or gathering myself, reminds me of our closeness to the earth and of our critical relationship with it.

Today I spend a good deal of time on another shore. The soft, rust brown, sandy beaches of the Northumberland Strait are much different from the craggy ominous waters I grew up knowing. In the spring, the sand flats are littered with men and women in rolled-up pants with buckets and shovels, ready to dig clams. Most of the clammers—like the mackerel fishers here—are going to enjoy the harvest at their own table. When the tide goes out on the Amherst Shore, you can walk for miles along the hard-packed sand. Its surface, molded by the waves, becomes a landscape of soft curves, undulating into each other. Although the sea appears to be a calm, easily controlled body of water, it is strong and powerful. I have watched how it quickly erodes the clay banks and have seen cottages tip into

LIVING ON THE EDGE OF THE EARTH
80" x 52" (2 x 1.3 m)

When you see picturesque coastal villages, it is easy to believe that everything there is perfect and to feel that you would prefer that place to wherever you are. It might seem as if nothing could ever go wrong in such a place. In truth, these communities are like anywhere else. As the people there build their lives, they face the same struggles people face anywhere. There is no such thing as a place to escape to, because, wherever we go, we carry with us whatever we are trying to leave behind. These crooked houses represent the reality of our lives and the struggles we all face, as beauty shines around us.

the ocean. During a winter of good storms, you can lose as much as three feet of the shore side of your property as the waves wash away the clay banks. When riled up, the coastal waters can tip a boat as quickly as the open waters of the Atlantic Ocean.

It took me years to find inspiration in this shore. Its flatness reminded me of a pond or inland water. I missed the hard edges of the coast I grew up with. Eventually, though, I became as charmed with periwinkles and hermit crabs as I was with barnacles. I watched my children grow on this shore, wading knee-deep in bathing suits. I have seen women grow older, and thicker, some wearing the same bathing suit for twenty years. It is a shore about the tides, and when you live there, you set your clock by them. When the tide is full you can swim. When it goes out six hours later, the basin empties and you can walk for miles on the sand flats. In between, you watch the water. Amherst Shore for me has become about bathing suits, dragonflies, summer rain, and wildflower fields. It is in every starfish and every little pitched roof cottage that I hook.

BONFIRE NIGHT
28" x 24" (71 x 61 cm)

I grew up in an Irish community, and, as teenagers, every November we celebrated Guy Fawkes Night (also known as Bonfire Night)—without having any idea of who Guy Fawkes was. It was all about the party!

FIELDS OF SUMMER

49" x 28" (1.2 m x 71 cm)

Whenever I see a field of summer flowers,
I feel like rushing into it and falling upon
it. It seems as if the softness of the petals
and colors would catch me before I felt the
ground beneath them.

There is a field on the Fenwick Road above my house from which I can see another body of water—the Bay of Fundy. I sometimes go there to watch how the bay swallows up parts of the Tantramar Marsh at high tide. I find colors that still surprise me. The bay has taught me how close brown is to mauve, how rich and deep its black-brown mud is. Driving to Rockport, New Brunswick, along the coastal road, littered with old, collapsing homesteads, I have watched the blues change to lavender. I hike at Fort Beausejour so I can watch the layers of blue and mauve shift as I get closer to the water. The water is one color as I walk toward it and another as I leave.

Many people have been caught off guard along the Bay of Fundy, doubting the speed at which the tide comes in and becoming trapped on a sandbar or cliff, in need of rescue. When I get to Advocate Harbour, I feel at home, because the bay suddenly becomes familiar, with its big, round rocks, open sea, and dark trees all around. This is the kind of water I know from childhood and it always makes me feel at home.

THE SALTWATER DANCE
48" x 30" (1.2 x 0.76 m)

Many of my friends have moved away for what they thought would be a few years only to find that they were going to spend a lifetime away. Sometimes, someone from "away" will unwittingly say, "Do you realize what you have here?" as if we were unaware of our surroundings. I never take living on this coast for granted. The people who stay here have chosen to do so and, as a result, have had to make a few sacrifices. Living here, with the coast on all sides, gives me great joy.

THE LOOK OUT
48" x 30" (1.2 x 0.76 m)

You cannot live on the water and not watch it. It draws you in and captivates you. During the summers, if we see a boat in the strait we get out the binoculars. We speculate on what the people aboard are doing: Are they fishing, in trouble, or having a beer on the bow? As a child, my father could recognize the boats passing through Freshwater from a mile away. He knew the sound of their engines and the color of their stripe. He spent his early life fishing and knew well the small things that identify a fisherman.

Despite my caution and respect for the water, I am inspired by it and interested in the way the seacoast communities interact with the sea. I can spend a half-hour letting the tide lap over my legs or get lost counting the dots on the back of a star fish. I love the views from the shore, how the houses seem to overlap one another, as if they were built on top of each other instead of on their own small squares of ground. Lighthouses offer a comfort, a message telling you to come forward and everything will be okay. As I am hooking mats, I am drawn to the simple yet perfectly formed hulls of boats that bob along on the water and to the cliffs of the shore. The power of the sea inspires all of us and fills us with awe.

My rugs have been inspired by my life along the seacoast. I know no better subject, yet the sea and its forces are so great that I can only know it a little. Throughout the years, I have kept returning to the water, in my work and in my life. I still retreat to the coast for a good part of the summer, and each year I gain a little further understanding. In this book, I explore my life along the coast and show its impact upon my work. The rugs in this book are of no particular place, but they reflect the Atlantic Coast of Canada. They tell stories about the simple life of coastal people and their homes, their communities, and their relationship with the sea—people who believe they are affluent, not because of what they own, but because of where they are.

LOVE AND FORGIVENESS
28" x 65" (71 cm x 1.6 m)

My father had a wonderful capacity to make you feel loved even though he could not give you what you wanted from him. In that way, he had a gift. As children in an Irish Catholic community, we lived under the rule of the Church. I would wait for my father when he went into the priest's house to take the "pledge"—a promise he made to God that he would not drink again. As I waited in the car, I knew it was unlikely he would keep the pledge, but I had the hope of a child. Sometimes, he would not drink for a few weeks afterward. Other times, we would go straight to the bar on the American navy base near our town. I made this rug the winter my father died, realizing that in his breaking of promises he taught me about love and forgiveness. Losing my father, although he had been sick for years, shook my core, but the simple thrumming motion, the pulling of loop by loop while making this mat helped me work it out. This piece is now in the home of my sister, Sharon Perry.

AS SUMMER TURNS TO FALL
58" x 38" (1.5 x 0.96 m)

I love watching the seasons change and
the landscape transform itself. As the light
changes with each season, it has a painterly
quality, turning the fields from green to gold.

CHAPTER 2

How to Hook Mats and Rugs

There are thirty-three rug designs in this book, inspired by scenes of coastal living, which you can create for yourself, your friends, and family. You can copy the designs or simply let them inspire you to create your own designs. Change them or adapt them as you wish—in fact, I encourage you to do just that. Let your rugs express your own experiences and relationship with the ocean, shore, and landscape. Adapt the colors, sizes, and textures however you like. I have listed the amounts you'll need of each material to make the same size rug I made. I have also suggested a way to copy the rug patterns found on pages 114–127.

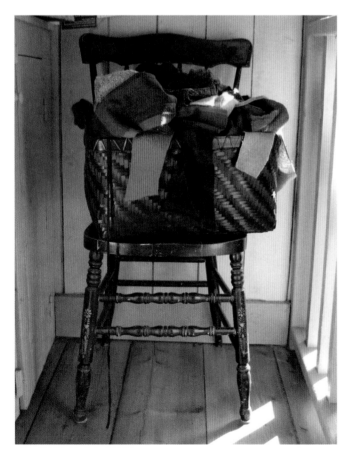

Part of the long rug-hooking tradition is to work with what you have. If your mother hooked rugs with T-shirts, you might want to, also. If your cupboard is full of leftover yarns or polar fleece, dig it out and put it to work. Make sure you like the feel of the materials you choose to hook. I have always worked with wool cloth, but recently I have been playing with different kinds of handspun yarns, silk jerseys, and other natural fibers. I like how they feel, and they are readily available to me. If all I had were my husband's old cotton-jersey pajamas, he'd be going to bed cold, because I would hook with those, too!

The tradition of rug hooking has never been about the material. It has been about self-expression, finding solace in hand work, and making the best of what you have. As you play with these designs, I hope you discover these qualities, which give rug hooking its true and lasting value and beauty.

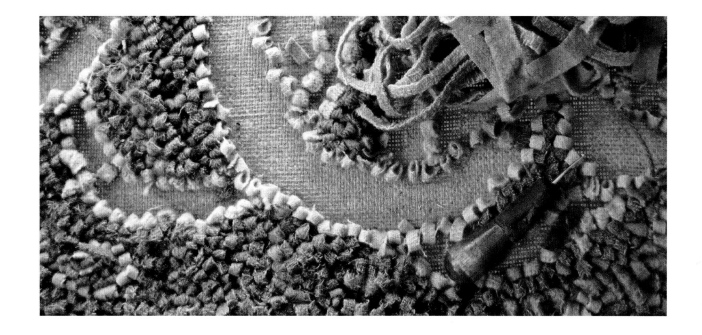

GATHERING FABRICS

There are absolutely no rules about what kind of materials you can hook into a rug. If you can cut it into a strip, you can hook it on to a backing. Once I was at a rug show in New Brunswick and noticed a particular rug. When I asked the coordinator of the show what material the artist used, she laughed and said, "Oh, she hooks potato-chip bags."

The easiest approach to rug hooking is to work with what you like and what is available to you. You may need to experiment with many different fabrics to find which ones feel best to you. I like natural fabrics such as silk, wool, and linen. I have even tried cotton velvet, but I find that it's rough on my hands. Many rug hookers work with cotton-jersey T-shirts, fleece, and cotton rags. There are even some mats made with strips of polyester and crimp knits.

When I am gathering fabric, I most often look for wool—the more texture to it, the better. I avoid thin, lightweight wool gabardines, but almost any other type of wool cloth is useful to me. I work with mohair scarves and throws, angora sweaters, merino or Shetland wool sweaters, old coats and skirts, long wool underwear and pants, and even blankets. These fabrics take dye easily and add wonderful textures to fields and skies. I am always on the lookout for cream-colored wools because they can be easily dyed to make any color. I also love bouclé fabrics because they are so good for hooking landscape.

Sweaters, long woolen underwear, even old woolen socks add a fluffy dimension to a hooked mat or rug. Very thin wools, such as serges and men's suiting, add a thready texture that is great for showing movement in the sea. Accent key areas of your design with bits of metallic fabrics or threads. Metallics draw the viewer's eye, so carefully choose where you place them to create impact and interest.

The first place to look for fabric is in your own closet. Ask family and friends what they have hanging around. The second place is in secondhand clothing stores. As soon as I come home with a load of clothing from the secondhand store, I throw it in the washer and dryer. I only want to work with clean fabric. I then tear out the linings, pull off the buttons and trims, and roll the cloth into bundles for storage.

When I shop for recycled clothing, I am drawn to wool skirts. They are so easy to take apart—and there are so many wool strips in them! Just cut off the waistband, remove the zipper, and you are ready to make and hook wool strips. Undo the pleats in a pleated skirt with a seam ripper, and you'll have yards of wool.

Storage is important. It is surprisingly easy to gather a good stash of fabric, but it is of no use to you if you cannot easily access it. Store your materials in an upright cupboard, on a shelf, or in a clear acrylic box or container so that you can see all the colors and textures available to you.

When I gather yarns, I generally look for handspun or hand-dyed wool yarns that are somewhat bulky and have two or more plies (twisted strands). I like yarn that has strands of several colors spun together or that change from thick to thin. Eyelash or bouclé yarns can add nice textures to your rug.

I also gather raw fleece, carded wools, and roving. These textures are great for making clouds and waves. They can also be dyed to make hair, bushes, flowers, or ocean accents. After it's washed, you can hook unspun wool—right off the sheep, llama, or goat—in its natural color or dyed. Spinners always have a vast array of yarns of different textures that will add interest to your work, so check with any you know or can find.

I am always on the lookout for fabric and yarns that I can use in my rugs. Nothing is too thick or thin to try. Keep your eyes open for materials that are available to you. Decide what you like to work with and use it confidently and freely.

CHOOSING BACKING

I have always preferred burlap as a backing for my rugs, but there are many backing choices. The backing material should be woven so you can easily pull the fabric or yarn strips through it. If the weave is too tight, you can strain or stress your hand. If the weave is too loose, you'll have trouble hooking fine strips. Be sure the backing suits the thickness of the fabric or yarn strips you're working with. If it does, you'll be able to relax as you work, and your finished project will be a success.

Primitive burlap—the choice of traditional rug makers—has a loose weave. It is excellent for hooking thick cloths and wide strips. Open-weave Scottish burlap is an excellent choice for hooking wider, thicker strips, which is what it is designed for. It is also good for finer, lighter weights of cloth. Some people prefer monk's cloth, which is 100 percent cotton and doesn't have the scratchy feeling of burlap, which some people don't like. Monk's cloth is also stretchier than burlap or linen and wears well. Linen is the premium rug backing. It is a strong backing that wears well and stands the test of time.

Make sure your backing is strong and in good condition. It is the foundation of your rug. The backing material should be relatively new. Don't work with backing that has been stored for years. The fibers may be weakened, and holes will appear seemingly out of nowhere. Keep your backing taut when you put it on the frame and as you hook to make the hooking easier and more comfortable.

TRANSFERRING PATTERNS

You'll find patterns for each of the projects on pages 114–127. The first step in transferring the pattern to your backing is to enlarge it on a photocopier to the size of the rug or mat you would like to make. To do this, you may need to photocopy parts of the pattern on several sheets of 11" x 17" (28 x 43 cm) paper and then tape them together to reconstruct the pattern at full size.

RESIZING PATTERNS

If you want to make any of these rugs in different sizes than suggested, simply resize the pattern by photocopying the pattern to size. Remember, for a larger size, you will need more wool than the amounts listed for the projects. A general rule of thumb is that you will need enough wool for four times the area that you want to hook. In other words, to hook an area that is 4" x 4" (10 x 10 cm), you will generally need a piece of cloth that is 16" x 4" (40 x 10 cm). This guideline will vary somewhat depending on the weight and thickness of the wool you are working with and on how tightly you hook—so be sure to allow a bit more just in case.

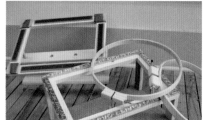

Transfer the pattern onto the backing of your choice with a red dot tracer, which is available at craft supply stores. Simply lay the red dot tracer over the pattern and trace the pattern with a black permanent marker. Then lay the red dot tracer on your backing material and trace it again with the permanent marker. The marker ink will seep through the red dot tracer onto your backing. When you have finished tracing the entire design, you can touch it up by directly drawing with your marker as needed.

PREPARING TO HOOK

To start hooking, you'll need a hook, a hoop or frame, and backing. Traditional hooks were made by driving a sharpened nail into a piece of wood, which was roughly carved to form a handle. Some were even made from old knives. There are many types of hooks on the market today. Some of the most common are the pencil-hook style with a long slim handle or the crochet-hook type on a standard 4" or 5" (10 or 13 cm) handle. Some people also find that they like to use different hooks for different textures. For example, you may want to work with one hook for cut cloth and another altogether for wool roving (unspun wool). The hooks themselves also come in a wide range of shapes and sizes, depending on the hooking material, but you should work with whatever tool you feel most comfortable with.

Choose a sturdy quilting hoop, a canvas stretcher (found at art supply shops), or a set of quilting or rug-hooking frames to hold your backing secure as you work. For larger pieces, you may want to work on a table frame.

You also need strands of fiber to form the loops—yarn, fleece, or any of the other materials discussed on pages 19–20. If you are working with fabric, be sure you launder it first. You'll also need to cut it into strips.

Cut strips that are about ¼" to ½" (6mm to 1.3 cm) long and about ⅛" to ¼" (3 to 6 mm) wide. Start with a rectangle of fabric that is about 8" x 4" (20.5 x 10 cm). Be sure the fabric has a straight edge. Fold the fabric four times accordion-style. Then cut strips parallel to the straight edge. It's best to work with 5½" (14 cm) scissors, which have short blades. Cut the strips as evenly as possible so they do not tear while you're hooking them through the backing.

HOW TO HOOK

Hooking rugs should be a relaxing, pleasant pastime. Before you begin, make sure that you are sitting in a comfortable position, your body is relaxed, and your back is supported. Take occasional breaks as you work, to avoid getting sore shoulders or hands. If you do, the hooking will go along much more easily and will be much more fun.

Put your pattern onto an embroidery frame or quilting hoop. It should lie flat and be tight, like the surface of a drum. As you hook, be sure to keep your burlap tight on your frame as this makes the hooking quite a bit easier.

Pick up the hook and hold it as you would hold a pencil, as shown in the photo at right. Hold a strip of yarn or fabric underneath the backing. It is a good idea to start by hooking an outline around a shape near the center of your pattern. Push the hook through a hole in the burlap and wrap the strip around the hook on the underside of the burlap. Lift the end of the strip up through the hole and leave it on the top of the backing.

Push the hook back down through a nearby hole in the backing. Catch the strip and slowly lift it to form a loop on the top surface of the backing, as shown in the second photo at right.

Repeat the process with the same strip of fabric, pulling it up loop by loop along the outline of your pattern. If you have trouble pulling up a strand, wiggle the hook back and forth slightly to widen the hole a little. Your loops should be ¼" to ⅓" (6 to 8 mm) high—but it doesn't matter if they're not all exactly the same height.

Continue to hook in every second or third hole of the burlap, depending on the width and thickness of your fabric. Make sure the surface is completely covered and there are no gaps where the backing shows through on the front or back side, as shown in the bottom photo. When you have hooked almost all of the fabric, pull the end of the strip to the top side of your pattern.

You can hook in straight or curved lines. Be sure not to cross the paths of your fabric strips on the back of the pattern—this will make your rug bulky and messy and the loops easy to pull out. Rather than carrying a color across the back of the rug, clip the strip and start again in a new place.

Continue to hook, by outlining and filling in all the areas of your rug. Clip the end so that it is even with the height of your loops, as shown in the photo at left. Do not hook too tightly, or your mat will not lie flat. Packing the loops together will keep them from falling out, but if you pack them too tightly the rug will curl.

As you hook, try not to simply work from left to right. Instead, try to cover several different parts of the rug's area. This way, in case you should run short of a particular fabric, you can add more of a slightly different color without it being too noticeable. This effect may even enhance the primitive quality of your design.

I press both sides of my finished pieces with a hot iron and a wet cloth. This process, which is called blocking, evens out any uneven loops and gives the rug a finished patina.

FINISHING THE EDGES

There are many ways to finish the edges of a rug, but I favor two different methods: one for floor mats and rugs and another for wall hangings. For both methods, leave a 2" (5 cm) border of excess burlap around your drawn pattern. You should never cut the backing too close to the edge of your hooking, or the hooked stitches may unravel.

If you are making a rug or mat for the floor, create an edge binding with black cotton twill tape. Hand-sew the tape around the outside edges of the backing with small stitches, as shown in the second photo at left. You can hook right up to the edge of the tape. When you've finished hooking the rug, roll the excess burlap into the twill tape. Then hand-sew the tape along the back side of your rug. This binding creates a small, slightly rounded edge all around the rug, which prevents the backing edges from wear. As an alternative, I sometimes sew together long strips of 3" (7.5 cm)-wide wool cloth and attach it just as I would the twill tape.

If you are hooking a piece for the wall, you don't need the twill tape. After you finishing hooking, simply fold the excess burlap to the back side of the rug. Sew it in place with a natural-colored cotton quilting thread to create a finished edge, as shown in the bottom photo.

To hang the hooked canvas, lay the top of the finished edge over a row of tacks—you don't need to put any nails through the rug. I like this method of mounting because I like the way the finished rug looks when framed by the wall instead of a black binding. Some rug hookers prefer a more decorative edge binding.

They may add a row of braiding, crochet, or yarn stitches around the border of their rugs. I prefer simple methods that allow the attention to focus on the hooking itself.

If you are hooking small, shaped, decorative projects—such as Christmas ornaments, magnets, and coasters—you can create an easy binding with glue. When you finish hooking your project, clip the strand ends and press the piece, with a wet cloth and a hot iron. Spread white glue over the entire backing. Let the glue dry overnight. The next day, simply cut away the excess burlap, and the hooked loops will stay securely in place. Do not use this method for any piece larger than a coaster—it's strictly for small, decorative items that would be too bulky with any other type of edge binding.

EXPERIMENTING WITH COLOR

Each of the projects has a color key of suggested colors for the design. You can work with these colors or you can experiment by including some of your favorite shades. You can also create a shaded effect by mixing two or three similar colors and hooking them randomly within a certain area. Don't be afraid to change the sky to a night sky or make the background darker or lighter. Color is a personal statement. Put your individual stamp on the rug you are making.

To begin, pull out the wools you have and lay them together on the burlap. Experiment with what looks good in the drawn pattern. Pull away the colors that do not work and substitute new ones. One simple way to create a color scheme is to choose a plaid or tweed that you like and use the solid colors in the plaid as the basis of the color plan for your rug.

Remember, if you change your mind about a color, you can always unhook it and try another. If you're having trouble deciding, rather than continuing to hook and rehook, simply move to another area of the pattern and work there for a while. Sometimes focusing on a different area will help you to work out the color problem more easily.

When I am designing rugs, I like to create fabric mixes. To create a water mix, I lay many different blues together on my table frame. I start with one or two bundles of cut strips, and then I add more colors one at a time, examining the ways in which the additions change the mix. If the change is good, I leave it. If the new color is not working, I remove it. Each color changes the mood or feeling of the mix to some degree. I work in the same way with green, taupes, and other colors to create landscape mixes. This process gives youa good idea of how the colors will work together when you have hooked them onto your backing.

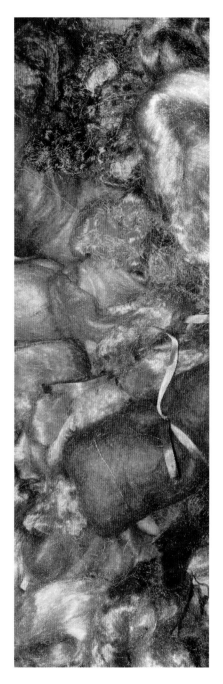

COLOR MIXES FOR SPECIAL EFFECTS

NIGHT SKY

When I begin to design a night sky for a mat, I imagine the northern lights, fireflies, and bonfires on the beach, and then the colors start to dance in my head. Instead of relying on straight navy blue, I imagine the color mixed with royal blues, blacks, purples, and greens, highlighted with mauves and teals.

FACES

I rely mainly on a mixture of light, medium, and dark shades of camel and tan, often working with several shades in each face. Naturally, you would adjust the mixture depending on the race of the person you are depicting. I do not clearly distinguish facial features. Instead, I select the lightest or darkest shades of the wools I am working with to simply create the impression of features.

DAYTIME SKY

The color you select for the sky depends on the type of day you are portraying. For a gray or foggy day, you might mix several shades of gray with a gray tweed. For a sunny day, mix several shades of clear light blue with some white, unspun, natural sheep's wool. Natural-colored unspun sheep's wool makes great skies. White is great for large cumulus clouds, and shades of blues and grays add liveliness and natural movement. You can mix both grays and blues for weather that is slightly untrustworthy.

HOUSES

I approach a hooked house as if it were my own and I were about to paint it. I outline the house in a solid color and then fill it in with another solid color. I will often use tweeds or dark shades for the roof. I think it's great fun to hook the insides of the outlined windows with bits of interesting yarns or tweeds in colors that pick up the main colors of the rug or mat. There's great beauty in the details!

SNOW

For snow, I mix two or three different shades of white-to-cream wool with the palest of blues, greens, and aquas. To add sparkle and texture, I often throw in a bouclé yarn or a shimmery white yarn with a bit of metallic.

FLOWER GARDENS

For flowers, I like to use unspun sheep's wool dyed in a multitude of colors. Pull up loops of bright pink, gold, red, and blue. Accent them with a bit of green. When you step away from your rug, you'll see how your garden has grown.

THREE-BAG METHOD FOR LANDSCAPE

I have an approach I call the Three-Bag Method for Landscape. First, sort your fabric strips into light greens, medium greens, and dark greens. Put each pile into a separate bag. Take a handful from the first bag and put it in the second bag. Take a handful from the second bag and put in the third bag. Work with the bag of light greens for the foreground of the scene. Work with the bag of medium greens for the middle of the landscape, filling areas between the light greens in the foreground. Work with the bag of dark greens to hook the back hills. Choose other colors to add texture or to create rocks and other design elements within the landscape. What would happen if you put a bit of purple in the back hills or a bit of royal blue? You will just have to try it to find out.

WORKING WITH TEXTURE

Passionate rug hookers love playing with texture. The process is an invitation to explore touch, the most sensual aspect of hooked rugs. Texture adds dimension and depth that can give a flat rug interesting sculptural qualities, encouraging the viewer to reach out and feel the fibers. Somehow, texture also makes a hooked design seem more lifelike and picturesque. Plaids and tweeds create the appearance of regular surface textures. Soft, heavily textured wools—such as hand-spuns, slubs, natural sheep's wool, carded wool, bouclé, and heavily textured cloth—add warmth and extra dimension. Bits of silk, linen, and even fine bits of metallic cloth can turn an otherwise ordinary rug into an original work of art.

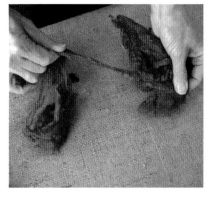

You hook most textured fibers just as you would hook any type of cloth or yarn. Before working with natural sheep's wool, I pull it gently into a 5" to 6" (12.5 to 15 cm) strip, as shown in the photo at right. Then I hook the strip as I would a cut strip of cloth. I also pull the fiber to form a higher loop while hooking, so it stands out from the rest of the loops on the surface of the rug.

If you are working with a fine yarn or very thin fiber, it's a good idea to hook several strands together to make the fibers more pronounced within the design. If you want the fiber to recede or blend into the background, just hook it as a single strand. It will create a finely textured effect.

Textured fibers, whether dyed or natural, will add a variety of special effects to your rug and mat designs. Natural unspun sheep's wool makes great clouds and big, fluffy ocean waves. Dyed blue, it makes an expanse of billowing sky or sea. Sometimes, I hook three textures in large patches to emphasize the effect. If you hook the wool in thin, spindly lines, the sky will look as if it is partially hidden by clouds. Hook rows of unspun wool under the crest of waves to highlight them and add drama.

To add texture to landscape, you can work with almost anything, in nearly any shade. Golds, rusts, and other autumn shades are perfect for showing the fall season or a parched terrain. Bright yellows, reds, and purples make flowers "pop." Greens add dimension in the surface of trees, bushes, and land. I particularly like multicolored slub because the variegated quality changes the look of the land.

It's very important to practice working with texture, so you will have a better understanding of what your materials can do. As you work with different types and varieties of wool, for example, you'll learn how each one looks when it's hooked into a design. You'll also learn how to gain greater control over the material and make it work for you. Try everything, even if you think it might not be quite right. Push your limits and sometimes override what you think may be your better judgment. This approach will increase your ability to work with a variety of fibers and will also allow you to put your own creative stamp on your work. Remember, you can always pull it out if it's not working and just start again! Hooking has a very forgiving nature.

DESIGNING YOUR OWN RUGS

The first step in the design process is to think about the look and shape of your rug. Answer the basic questions below, and you should have a good idea of the type of rug you want to make:

· Am I making this rug for a particular place?

· Am I making it just for fun and will decide where to put it later?

· How big do I want it to be?

· What shape do I want it to be?

· Do I want to include a border?

· What are my favorite colors? Should I choose these or create a specific color scheme?

· What look am I after? Do I want a rug that is "folksy," whimsical, serious, primitive, subtle, or something else?

Keep a basket to catch all the bits and pieces that are left over from each rug. An old basket near my hooking chair gives me a place to put all these little treasures and ensures that nothing is wasted.

Designing your own rug is simple—especially if you work with templates. A template is a cutout or stencil of a design motif. If you work with templates, you can design rugs even if you don't know how to draw. You simply create a paper template and trace its shape onto your backing fabric.

At the turn of the century, and perhaps earlier, women carefully saved the brown paper wrapping of store-bought goods and made templates for their rugs and mats. They would copy a design off a favorite china cup, for example, or trace the rose off the stamped pattern bought from a peddler so they could use it over and over again in different ways. Templates are not new. They are a time-honored tradition and as much a part of rug hooking as the so-called "stamped back" patterns drawn or stenciled onto burlap.

The simplest way to work with templates is to cut them out and use them exactly as they are. If you would like to make a rug with larger motifs, you can also enlarge the template designs on a photocopier and cut them out at their new size. Trace your templates onto stiff cardboard, clear plastic, or other materials so that you can keep your original patterns in good condition for future use.

Feel free to work with the motifs in the projects to create your own original designs for yourself, family, and friends (remember, the designs are protected from resale by copyright).

Simply photocopy the motif to make a template. Cut out the template and lay it on your backing wherever you'd like to create a new design. Then trace the template with a permanent marker to create your own "stamped" pattern to hook. Always draw your patterns on the backing with a good permanent-ink marker that will not bleed. I like the Sharpie brand permanent markers. When drawing a design with templates, I work with both a red and a black permanent marker to help me distinguish between elements in the foreground and elements in the background.

Mix motifs from different patterns to create your own designs. For example, the woman in *Woman on the Path* (page 97) could be standing on the shore waiting for The *Cape Islanders and Dories Coming Ashore* (page 92). Lay the templates for the various motifs directly on the backing. Move them around to configure different designs and choose what you like before you trace them.

Another way to approach the design process is arrange and trace the templates onto a large sheet of paper. When you have a design you like, follow your drawing to reposition and trace the templates onto your backing.

You can also draw directly onto the backing. If you change your mind about the design, you can always simply turn over the backing material and start again on the other side. Rug hooking is a forgiving craft—it gives you a second chance right from the start.

LETTERING

Written words or phrases that you'd like to add become part of the rug's design and composition, so it is important to plan their placement. The border of the mat usually works well for written elements.

Be sure the words that you choose relate to the subject of the mat and are meaningful. I avoid adding dates, names, or any specific statements that too directly personalize the mats. I prefer to choose words and phrases that make the mat more interesting and draw in the viewer. I also like to write in my own handwriting to add a personal touch.

The process is simple. Decide what you want to write—maybe a great quote or a saying or sentiment of your own. Next, choose where you want to place it in the design. Write the words on the surface of the backing with a permanent marker. You can hook the writing just as it is written or with a double line of hooking, so that the lettering stands out. If I want the words to be clearly legible, I make sure there is a strong contrast between the color of the words and the background color. Sometimes I am happy to have the words be very subtle within the design. In this case, I choose similar colors for the lettering and background.

CARING FOR HOOKED MATS AND RUGS

Hooked rugs and mats are strong, and they should last for years if you take good care of them. The weakest part of the mat is often the backing. In fact, many people prefer a linen backing because the fiber is stronger.

Many of the old mats that our grandmothers made long ago have disintegrated. My Aunt Mary once told me that her least-favorite childhood chore was taking the family's hooked rugs down to the wharf to clean them, first by dipping them in saltwater and then beating them before hanging them over a fence to dry. No wonder there are so few left around!

Never soak or immerse a hooked mat or rug in water. I don't dry-clean mine either. If a mat gets a spot on it, I clean the surface with a damp cloth and gentle soap, making sure the cloth is not so wet that it soaks through the mat. Often, if a mat needs freshening, I wait for a new snowfall and lay the mat upside down in the new snow for a gentle surface cleaning.

CHAPTER 3

Welcome Mats

Welcomes to my childhood home most often involved welcoming home Newfoundlanders who had gone away to Labrador, Ontario, or to the United States to find work. Most often, these visitors were relatives or the children of neighbors who returned each summer to their home. The welcomes were simple. Most often, my mother would lay out the table before the guests arrived. Those coming at lunchtime were greeted with thinly sliced ham, pickles, cheddar cheese, homemade bread and tea, and raisin buns. The foods were laid upon a saucer on the table and mugs of tea were handed to every guest. It was only when these guests came to the house that my mother would put a cloth on the table. The rest of the time she covered the table with bright squares of oilcloth that could be easily wiped and cleaned.

As a small child, I was famous for visiting the neighbors. During these visits, I learned a lot about welcomes. By the time I was eight years old, my sisters had all moved away from home, so the house was quiet. I would often go visit my mother's friends. We always referred to our neighbors by their first name, with a Mr. or Mrs. in front of it: Mrs. Anne, Mrs. Eileen, Mrs. Bride, Mrs. Edna, and Mrs. Kitty were our closest neighbors. I visited people each day, making my rounds as if I were an old woman myself. I would sit with the women in their kitchens as they prepared their dinners or sat crocheting. I was often welcomed with a peppermint knob or a homemade cookie.

There is a touristy welcoming tradition for visitors to Newfoundland called "kissing the cod." After drinking Screech (a Jamaican rum) and kissing a cod fish, a visitor is deemed an honorary Newfoundlander. There was never such a thing in a real Newfoundland house—any cod of a decent size was fried for supper and its head was stewed with onions, potatoes, and carrots for the next day's lunch.

Welcomes are not about rituals. They are about cultivating relationships so that people know they are where they should be. A good coastal welcome is based on making a person feel glad to have come. Welcomes are about storming the kettle and pouring the tea. These days we have become dependent on things that distract us and keep our minds busy. Visiting has become harder to do. We sit at home at night in front of the television or the computer. The thought of just dropping in to visit someone seems unrealistic. The truth is, around here anyway, all you need to say is, "I just came for a visit," and most everyone will understand and step aside so you can walk in the door.

Starting small can lead to big things. These welcome projects are a great size for a welcome mat, a small, framed wall hanging, or a chairpad. In primitive rug hooking, anything smaller than 10" x 10" (25.5 x 25.5 cm) is hard to work because it is difficult to maneuver big stitches in a small piece. The beauty of rug hooking is that there is only one stitch to learn—so if you are good at starting what you finish, you don't have to worry. You can make these projects as large as you like.

KISSING FISH WELCOME 2
12" x 24" (30.5 x 61 cm)

A good coastal welcome is about making people feel glad they came. It is about the preparation of good food made with love and about knowing that there will be good fun and that the visit will strengthen and deepen a friendship.

MATERIALS

- ¹/₃ yard (30.5 cm) total of various dark blues
- ¹/₈ yard (11.4 cm) green
- ¹/₈ yard (11.4 cm) dark rust
- ¹/₈ yard (11.4 cm) gold
- ¹/₈ yard (11.4 cm) black

Living on the Edge
10" x 12" (25.5 x 30.5 cm)
(Pattern, page 114)

This rug design grew out of a workshop I did on hooking the night sky. I wanted to show participants how to express movement, madness, light, and depth in the midnight sky. It was an exciting project because of the large area of sky in each rug. Participants had room to play around and they used the movement of their hooking and the various shades in the sky to be expressive.

Remember that the sky is not always blue. When hooking a mat, you can make the sky any color you want. Look closely at the greens and reds in the sky. Perhaps the Northern Lights are peeking through. I chose colors similar to the sky colors to fill in the windows to give the house a hollow, free-floating feeling, as if it were slipping off the edge of the earth. Living on the coast often feels like living on the edge of the world. People don't stay here because it is easy, but because they want to.

Wish Upon a Starfish

10" x 10" (25.5 x 25.5 cm)

(Pattern, page 115)

This little rug is simple to make. You need a few cream and white strands tossed together. Select variegated yarn to show the details of the prickly skin of the starfish. You can outline your fish in the same dark blue color in the border. Hook the background in a circular motion to create the swirling effect of a tidal pool.

MATERIALS

- $1/4$ yard (22.9 cm) blue
- $1/4$ yard (22.9 cm) off white
- $1/8$ yard (11.4 cm) dark blue
- Scraps for the markings on the starfish

"Along the beach there are small pools in the rocks that have small starfish only a few inches (centimeters) wide. I like to look at them, lying on top of each other, another rug in the making."

Materials

- ¹⁄₄ yard (22.9 cm) brown for the moose
- ¹⁄₈ yard (11.4 cm) gold for lettering
- ¹⁄₈ yard (11.4 cm) total of various forest greens for trees
- ¹⁄₈ yard (11.4 cm) total of various light greens for grass
- ¹⁄₈ yard (11.4 cm) rust for earth
- ¹⁄₂ yard (45.7 cm) total of various dark blues and navy for sky
- Scraps of yellow, white, ivory, tan, medium blue, and black yarn for outlining

SHAPED RUGS

When designing shaped rugs, be sure that your edges are not so sharp and jagged that they are impossible to bind. Also, consider whether an unusual shape suits the subject. A shaped edge looks best if it depicts some aspect of nature that has a defined edge—such as a tree line or the soft hills behind a village.

Moose Welcome

25" x 7" (63.5 x 18 cm)

(Pattern, page 115)

When you hook the night sky in this rug, try hooking in the medium blue yarn first, working in curvy, organic lines. Create scattered stars by simply hooking one or two loops of yellow, cutting the strip, and then starting in a different area. It will look like you are hooking small polka dots all over the sky area of the mat. You can then randomly hook in the blue and navy strips around the stars and curvy lines to give your sky some movement and depth.

"When I was little, my father hunted moose. He was always telling stories about the big bull moose he got—or better still, the one that got away."

THE MEANING OF THE JOURNEY
48" x 27" (1.22 x 0.69 m)

If I spend too much time trying to figure out the meaning of
life, I get confused. There are so many questions that I cannot
answer, so many things I do not understand. I am left to think
that the meaning of our journey is defined by those we travel
with through it. It is our love for others and our joy in caring
for one another that will matter at our end. It is the bit of fun
and devilment, the dance in the kitchen on a Saturday night,
and the keeping busy that enriches us. Sometimes, we need
to be the man in the door watching what is going on, but
there are times when we need to join the dance.

Babes on the Beach
16" x 34" (40.5 x 86.5 cm)

I love a woman who wears her bathing suit proudly and comfortably regardless of a few extra pounds or a sagging this or that. The older I get, the more beauty I see in age and character. I am finding it a much more interesting kind of beauty than the beauty of youth. It used to be I couldn't tell gray-haired women in glasses apart from one another. Now I find that I cannot tell one perfectly coiffed blond-haired young woman with French tips from another.

Seashell Welcome

15" x 7" (38 x 18 cm)

(Pattern, page 116)

When you hook this rug, hook the shells from the middle out in a circular motion in order to emphasize the shape of the moon snail. You will follow the swirl of the snail, so to speak.

Enhance the swirl with bits of taupe or mauve so that it becomes more noticeable. I like to use this swirl shape to add a little interest in the background. Flat backgrounds are not much fun to hook and they can make the rug look a bit stiff. I like to use colors that make me "feel" the sea: light shades of blues, mauve, lavender, and pink mixed with creams. This rug can be hooked in many different combinations of sea-inspired colors.

Although you can work with the pattern exactly as shown, it would be a great idea to write the "welcome" in your own handwriting, making it more of a personal greeting that you can hang over your door. This rug could also be enhanced with a bit of metallic thread hooked in the background to approximate shimmering sand.

MATERIALS

- $1/2$ yard (45.7 cm) total of various whites and palest mauve or gray for shells and background

- $1/8$ yard (11.4 cm) dark blue green for outlining

- $1/8$ yard (11.4 cm) total of various light blues for highlights

- $1/8$ yard (11.4 cm) total of various mauves for lettering

MATERIALS

- $1/4$ yard (22.9 cm) total of mixed reds for fish

- $1/2$ yard (45.7 cm) total of mixed dark navy and royal blues for background

- $1/4$ yard (22.9 cm) total of mixed gold or yellows for lettering

- $1/8$ yard (11.4 cm) royal purple for border

- $1/8$ yard (11.4 cm) pale green for outlining

- Scraps and details: pink eyes, pink, mauve, blue green for spots on fish; wine to outline letters

Kissing Fish Welcome

24" x 10" (61 x 25.5 cm)

(Pattern, page 116)

It seems you can't go wrong putting certain colors together. Blue, red, and yellow make a good combination if you want a spirited feeling to your rug. (Fish that kiss certainly must be spirited!) Yellow always seems to jump off royal blue. The color of the lettering needs to contrast with the background color of the rug if you want to be able to read the word "welcome" in the rug. Make the gills a little curvy to give the fish some spunk and attitude.

"I often hook red fish because I like the term 'red herring,' which the dictionary defines as an irrelevant diversion. Many good visits start out as irrelevant diversions. Plans get in the way of letting things just happen."

There is a Place Where the Fishermen Gather

8' x 6' (2.4 x 1.8 m)

Making this rug taught me a lot about inspiration and how to let the mood of the moment and what is happening around you play a part in your rug design. As I lay on the floor sketching a new rug, I heard news on the radio about recent happenings in the local fishery. I decided to add elements to the village scene I was sketching that were relevant to the news coming over the airways. I wrote in the border, "There is a place where the fishermen gather"—a line from an old folk song, which seemed to suit the subject and also described this great place to be.

GATHERING TOGETHER

When rug hookers gather—as they often do for hook-ins—the event usually includes good food, and of course, strong tea. It is a natural part of being together to share a meal and share recipes. These traditional oatcakes go a long way. They make a great lunch served with a piece of aged cheddar.

Mrs. Sanford's Nova Scotia Oatcakes
3 cups (240 g) oats
3 cups (375 g) flour
1 cup (200 g) sugar
1 cup (225 g) butter, at room
    temperature
1 cup (200 g) shortening
1/4 cup (60 ml) water
1/2 teaspoon salt

Mix all ingredients together and work the mixture into the softened butter and shortening. Roll out the mixture to 1/4" (6.5 mm) thickness and cut into circles with a drinking glass. Bake at 375°F (200°C) for 15 minutes. Serve with maple butter, honey, or cheddar cheese and Red Rose tea.

CAPTAIN'S HOUSE
12" x 24" (30.5 x 61 cm)

In every community, there are a few houses that once belonged to someone great, whose story lives on through the house. Every time people pass, they acknowledge the life of that person from long ago.

THE FERRY TERMINAL

36" x 16" (91.5 x 40.5 cm)

Without a doubt, island life involves a ferry. I grew up waiting for people to come in on the ferry and bringing people down to catch the ferry. My sisters would arrive home from the mainland. My aunt would return for her annual visit from Brooklyn, New York, where she ran boarding houses. Her station wagon would be packed full of kids and summer gear. It was part of a good welcome to be there to greet them and to wave them off from the dock as they left. In this 1994 rug, I am showing the good-byes, the last few words shared between the women, the final nod of the head between the men.

CHAPTER 4

Old-Fashioned Mats

Rug hooking has always been a coastal pastime. It is a craft indigenous to North America, having sprung up somewhere along the eastern seaboard or in Quebec in the early to mid-nineteenth century. No doubt it was derived from the "proddy," or poked, style of hooking that had been going on in England for centuries, which involved poking rather than hooking scraps of fabric up through burlap. The poked style is still common in England and also on Tancook Island off the coast of Nova Scotia.

Since it began, rug hooking has been considered a pastime or utilitarian craft—something women did in the kitchen—more than an art. The truth is, however, that for more than a century women having been putting art into their rugs. Only the relatively well-to-do could afford to order stamped patterns from a catalog. The others had to create their own. Most often, they worked with a bit of charcoal from the fire to "mark off" a simple geometric pattern or draw a design of scrolls and flowers onto a brin (burlap) sack that had once held potatoes or animal feed.

As is often the case among folk artists, the women shared with and copied from each other. If one woman could draw well, she would draw for the others, as my own grandmother did. Her neighbors would come over to ask her to draw their husbands' boats for them to hook. Some would improvise and adapt the stamped patterns in the catalogs to create new designs for their own parlors. Rug hookers have been creating art for a long time.

Through the years, as I have demonstrated rug hooking in communities across the Atlantic Maritimes, I have run into hundreds of people who say, "My mother used to do that." Until the late 1940s, there was a mat on the go in nearly every Maritime household. Much later than that, old hooks could still be found hanging in the shed or at the back of a junk drawer. I am continually amazed at the number of people who still have their grandmother's or mother's hook. It seems that long after the old woman had given up her craft, she saved the hook just in case someone wanted to get back at it. These hooks, often handmade by the man

of the house, are small, compact souvenirs of the way things used to be. These tools—easy to hang onto, without taking up too much room—are strong visual reminders of the men who made them and the woman who used them.

Over time, I have gathered a collection of old hooks that have been discarded by families and sent to auction sales and antique stores. I hated to see them left sitting there when they had once been such an intimate part of someone's creative life. As a rug hooker, I felt that they deserved a bit of prestige, so I formed a small collection. I gather them still as I make my way around the countryside. Some are made from knives and a bit of wood—one from a piece of brass pipe, another from a bullet. Some have carved initials so they would not be lost or misplaced, proving that a favorite hook is a valuable thing to the owner. As rug hooking has experienced a revival, these artifacts have become rare and a bit more expensive.

When I first started rug hooking, I visited a ninety-year-old woman, Mrs. Marlon Bird, who had moved to a small apartment from her big country farmhouse. When she heard that I hooked rugs, she said I should come back to her apartment for tea, that she had something to show me. Mrs. Bird was a small bright-eyed woman with white hair. At ninety, she was as interested in me as I was in her. After serving tea and ginger snaps, she took me to her living room where she kept a black trunk. It looked like a treasure chest and was full of finely embroidered linens, quilts, and her mother's blue willow china. It was Mrs. Bird's keeping place.

As she lifted out each item, she told me a little about it, until she finally found what she had been looking for: a manila envelope filled to the brim with old mat patterns of scrolls and flowers. They had been simply drawn and cut out of brown-paper grocery bags and butcher's paper. They were folded, creased, and

BLESSING OF THE BOATS
48" x 21" (1.2 x 1.53 m)

Fishing is a dangerous life, and everyone in a fishing community knows the perils of the sea. Each year, the boats are blessed before the fishing season begins.

wrinkled with age and wear. The edges were lined with black ink made as Mrs. Bird, her friends, and family had laid them on burlap and time and again traced them to make rugs. She told me that she had long ago quit hooking but she kept the patterns just in case.

The templates in the treasure trunk were among the few things saved from a lifetime of collecting, a reminder of the value of an art or craft to the creator. For rug hookers, the worth is not always in the finished product but instead in what the rug gives them as they make it.

My own life as an artist was an accidental journey. I never set out to spend my life creating hooked mats. I completed a master's degree in education, specializing in counseling, at Acadia University. The year I graduated, 1990, was also the year I learned to hook rugs. About two years later, I discovered that I could use this art form to express ideas and tell stories. This discovery captivated me. I have also discovered that teaching people to hook rugs has been as useful to some as the counseling I might have offered if my life had taken its initial path. Getting lost in any craft, using one's hands to create something tangible, is healthy for the soul. This experience makes rug hooking a powerful medium. I was lucky enough to find this out early on.

As much as I like to create a wonderful rug as a piece of art for the wall, there is something eminently satisfying about making a rug for the floor. Through the years, I have made many mats for the floors of my farmhouse. There have been hit-and-miss door mats, long hall runners, floor carpets, and bath rugs. I have played with traditional designs and more playful modern and funky styles.

For floor rugs, I have most often taken my inspiration from the traditional designs developed more than a hundred years ago. I live in a 165-year-old Georgian-style farmhouse, so the floors beg for traditionally inspired designs. When I put more contemporary designs on these old floors, I feel as if I am trying to make the house be something it is not. So I have given in to the house and dressed its floors in scrolls and primitive flowers. In spite of my home's demands, I love to play with bright exciting colors and twist the traditional ever so slightly, adding a modern edge. These modern rugs go off to other homes to be enjoyed.

Some of the rugs in this chapter are inspired by tradition. Others are inspired by the need to move away from it. As you hook these projects, feel free to play with the patterns, redesign them, and invigorate the spirit of hooking!

WASHING
52" x 42" (1.3 x 1.1 m)

I love the way women move as they work. It is almost as if you can see strength of character in the shape of their shoulders. Traditionally, rug hooking has been what a woman turned to when she needed to catch her breath and get some peace of mind. I find the thrumming of the hook almost meditative. Once I begin, I get lost in the color and feel of the wool, and the sliding of it between my fingers. It is a practice of enchantment.

ANTIQUE FLORAL RUG (above)
24" x 48" (61 cm x 1.2 m)

ORIGINAL NEWFOUNDLAND RUG (right)
24" x 38" (61 x 96.5 cm)

These two antique rugs are quite different.
The traditional rose and scroll rug, shown
above, was most likely hooked on a stamped
pattern. This means that the design was
predrawn on a burlap backing. The rug at
right was found in a home in Newfoundland.
It is an original design. The maker was most
likely inspired by the popular, biblical, lion-
and-lamb design, but chose to hook a small
dog in place of the lamb. The mansard roof is
typical of early Newfoundland architecture.
These are both historically important rugs.

Coming Home
42" x 30" (1.1 m x 76 cm)

The return home happens for many of us at one time or another. We build a life somewhere else and then take some time before we return to the place where we grew up. What we find when we get there changes, depending on our age or the stage of our lives.

WATCHING OVER

20" x 28" (51 x 71 cm)

The birth of a child is one of the most life-altering experiences in a parent's life. You become a keeper of someone else rather than a keeper of yourself.

Old-Time Leaves in the Border

70" x 50" (1.8 x 1.3 m)
(Pattern, page 117)

When you hook a large rug like this, make sure you have plenty of wool. Look for many different shades of each of the background colors so that, if you begin to run short, you can introduce yet another shade without it being too obvious.

Before I start, I cut up only half of my total amount of material. When it begins to get low, I will know whether or not I need to introduce more colors or if I will have enough to complete the project. The general rule is that you need four times the amount of material than the area you are going to hook. The amount will vary depending on how high you hook your loops and how wide your strips are.

I also am careful never to completely hook an area from left to right without considering how much fabric I have. If you completely hook in an area with just a few fabrics and you run out when you have only a few inches (centimeters) left to hook, it will be very difficult to match the colors. In this case, you will have to undo some of your hooking throughout that area and introduce a new color so that it blends in. For this reason, I never like to hook a large area in a solid color—and also because it gets quite boring to hook the same color over and over again. Backgrounds hooked in a single solid color can look very flat and uninteresting. Mix it up!

MATERIALS

- 5 yards (4.5 m) total of various tans for background and outlining leaves and vines
- $1/2$ yard (45.7 cm) gold or caramel for lines around border and leaves
- $1/4$ yard (22.9 cm) rose and green plaid for leaves
- 1 yard (0.9 m) total of various greens for thin border around background and leaves
- 3 yards (2.5 m) total of various wines
- $1/8$ yard (11.4 cm) rose for corner flowers
- $1/8$ yard (11.4 cm) creamy yellow and gold for corner flowers

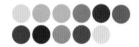

MATERIALS

- 3 yards (2.5 m) total of various tans and a little coral for center
- 2 yards (1.5 m) total of terra cottas and rust for inside border
- 3/4 yard (68.6 cm) green for scrolls
- 1/4 yard (22.9 cm) wines to outline scrolls
- 1/4 yard (22.9 cm) gold for centers of scrolls
- 2 yards (1.5 m) total of golden browns and copper for outside border
- 1/4 yard (22.9 cm) dull lavender or rose for scroll details
- 1/4 yard (22.9 cm) wine for scroll details
- 1/4 yard (22.9 cm) green and gold plaid for scroll highlights

Old–Time Scrolls

54" x 48" (1.4 x 1.2 m)
(Pattern, page 118)

Look for variegated wools, tweeds, and plaids for the scrolls. With some of the green, I hooked tendrils into the rust middle border to give a little more interest to this part of the background. The rusts and terra cotta go from light to medium dark, as do the tans and browns in the other background areas.

I enjoy playing with color in these border and background areas. I also find that scrolls look good when outlined in a dramatic color that is quite different from the shades in the scroll itself. The contrast allows you to easily emphasize the curl at the end of the scroll.

Although scrollwork is traditionally Victorian in design, I like the way it works in primitive-style rugs. The scrolls appear very organic, reminiscent of curled leaves, ferns, and vines. I have always been attracted to this type of design. In fact, my very first hooked mat had four scrolls in the corner and a few leaves around the border. Antique mats with scrolls around the border are commonly found throughout Atlantic Canada, and the pattern is still popular among contemporary rug hookers.

Gathering Grapes
5" x 5" (1.5 x 1.5 m)

Part of my summer life is spent looking out for the grapevines. I planted them as vines to climb up the front of the cottage, but also to have leaves to make rolled grape leaves, which we called Wa-ah Areesh. My husband's family is Lebanese, and the grapevine is an important part of their family culture. In July, as soon as the leaves are ready, we roll meat and rice into the leaves and serve them with generous helpings of homemade yogurt (leban). It is a part of the summer to sit on the front veranda, rolling up the little bundles. One day my mother-in-law told me that I was good at rolling the leaves because of all the rug hooking I'd done. There was a little sense of relief in her voice, knowing that her boy would continue to be fed Wa-ah Areesh.

THE CHURCH AND THE VILLAGE

12' x 6' (3.7 x 1.8 m)

This rug is the largest rug I have made so
far. Its colorful posy border is a tribute to the
strong tradition of rug hooking that exists
on the Atlantic Coast. The border of fish is a
reminder of what brought us here in the first
place. The rug is a reflection of the changing
role of the church in today's community, as
some people walk toward, others walk away,
and some manage to avoid it altogether.

MAKING IT BIG

When you make a large rug—more than 3' (0.9 m) in any dimension—there are important things to consider. First, make sure your backing is wide enough for the finished rug. You don't want to piece the backing because it is difficult to hook through two layers.

You also need to be sure you have enough wool to finish the project. The general rule is you need enough material to cover the area that you want to hook four times. Color planning is essential, too. If it's difficult to find enough material in one color, choose several colors that are very nearly the same shade.

Choose the right frame for the job before you start, too. A large rug can become very heavy—too heavy to hook on a lap frame. For large pieces, I work on a Cheticamp-style frame that has 80" (2 m) bars. A quilt frame also works well. Another important tip: Make sure that you find the design interesting, so you don't get bored and decide not to finish!

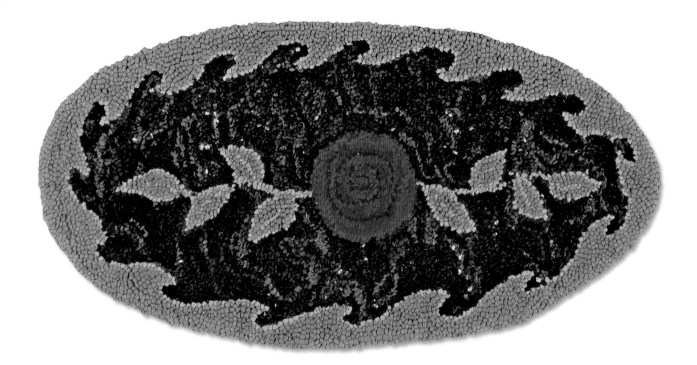

Old Rose Oval

48" x 20" (1.2 m x 51 cm)
(Pattern, page 118)

Try to find a black-and-wine tweed fabric so that you can pick up some of the red of the rose when you are hooking the background. One of the tweeds I used here had flecks of white in it, which gave the rug a very homespun look. If you want a more formal feeling for the rug, work with solid, dark fabrics.

The rose benefited from a very orange red. The color added dimension and made the rose look as if it were projecting in some areas. It also gave the petals a realistic effect. The rose itself is a simple swirl that starts with a C in the center. It's followed around three times to form a circle. The realistic effect comes from mixing the reds in the swirl so it looks like petals.

"To my mother, who learned to hook as a girl at my grandmother's knee, a mat was not much of a mat if it did not have a rose in it. Big cabbage roses are the central design in many traditional patterns. They most often had a dark or black background."

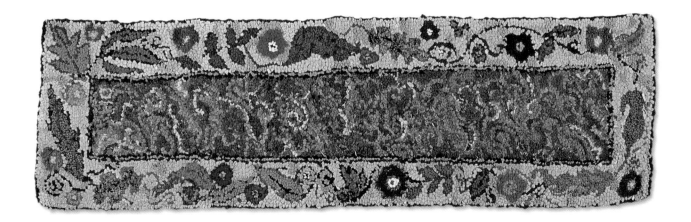

Antique Leaf Runner

70" x 20" (1.8 m x 51 cm)
(Pattern, page 119)

Outline some of the flowers in colors that contrast with what you plan to use in the flower bodies. Outline and fill some of the flowers in shades of the same color. This variation will give the posies an abandoned, unplanned look, which works well in primitive-style rugs.

Notice that the leaves are curled and that there are often tendrils coming from the vines that connect them. Blue-based forest greens are mixed freely with brown-based khaki greens to create a natural look.

This rug has a well-worn appearance that can only be had from years of use as a floor mat. It sits by the door for the children to wipe their boots off on. I appreciate how the loops are beaten down, making the surface of the rug flat rather than soft and cushy.

As people's time has become scarce, the mats they make are often hung on the wall as hangings. I do hang mats on the wall, and many of the rugs I make are used as artwork, but I still believe in mats on the floor, even mats by the door. I hate to think that this tradition is getting too highfalutin for its own roots. Practicality is a trait I really value, not just in mats, but in people, too.

MATERIALS

- 1 1/2 yards (1.4 m) total of medium, light, and dark browns for center
- 2 yards (1.8 m) total of various pale golds and taupes for border
- 1/2 yard (45.7 cm) total of various greens and green tweeds for leaves and vines
- 1/4 yard (22.9 cm) total of various pinks, wines, and roses for flowers and line around border
- 1/4 yard (22.9 cm) total of various reds and oranges for flowers
- 1/4 yard (22.9 cm) total of various blues for flowers and line around border
- 1/4 yard (22.9 cm) purple for flowers and line around border
- Scraps: various colors for flowers

CHAPTER 5

People and Places

Freshwater, Newfoundland—my hometown—was made up of people who had come there for their futures and those who had been torn away from their pasts. My father and mother gladly left behind what my father called "the slavery of the fishery" to work on the U.S. naval base at Argentia, where they were paid real cash, the first real money either of them had ever made. Many other families came to Freshwater much more reluctantly, having been pulled away from their outport homes as part of a resettlement program or forced to sell their land to make way for the navy base. Everyone made a go of it one way or another, although few really prospered. For some, there was greater yearning in their hearts for what they left behind than for anything that might come with a biweekly paycheck.

By the time I was born, a generation or two had been raised in the shadows of the navy base. It left its mark on everyone. Liquor was cheap, and gambling was easy. Husbands and sometimes wives would disappear for days on a bender. Most people lived, worked, and drank hard—but they loved easily and gave freely of themselves and whatever they had. Plenty of girls from our hill, including a couple of my sisters, moved away to the States with navy guys. Some did well, while others returned years later, tired and worn, with kids but no navy guy.

After my six sisters had all moved away, my father and mother decided to move, too—from Newfoundland to Nova Scotia. I didn't want to leave and spent my sixteenth summer wishing I could preempt it. My father, though, was hell-bent on leaving. My sister in Nova Scotia had had my parents' first grandchild, and my mother was to look after her while my sister worked. My father had a small pension from the base, and they would be able to make ends meet there.

I did not want to go, even though reality was staring me in the face. Mrs. Edna in the big red-and-white house next door had died. For several years, her house had been falling into disrepair. One evening as the light was going down, I was sitting on the stairway leading to the third floor of our house playing with the cream lace curtains. Through the two layers of glass, a regular window and the storm

window, which stayed on all year round to protect us from the pounding wind, I saw two rats scurrying about on the walk to Mrs. Edna's door. They were fearless in the daylight, just as if it were the town dump we were living next to and not the once brightly painted house that was filled with the scent of homemade bread and fish cakes. That moment has stuck with me all my life. I still shiver at the thought of the rats being so close to my own life. I knew we had to go, but I hated to leave.

I still love the hills, the creamy white and gray granite that crowd the fields of my home in Newfoundland. I have affection for squat spruce trees that can't get out of their own way. I can still feel the weight of the wind slapping the collar of my jacket hard against my face and the fog settling over the evening as I headed out the main road to meet my friends. I still love to see the people I grew up with there. There is an honesty between people who grew up together that leaves no room for pretense. If your father drank too much or your mother went to bingo every night or your brother was a thief, you both knew it. There is no hiding from who you are, and there is comfort in that.

When I visit Freshwater now, my memories of the past sometimes scrape against the realities of the present. It would be easy to fall into romantic notions wondering what if this or that hadn't happened, but, truthfully, there is always something happening, something changing in coastal communities. It is the character of the people, whether we leave or stay, that remains constant.

WATCHING OVER THE SHORE
60" x 32" (1.5 m x 81.5 cm)

Many of these little cottages along the Northumberland Strait have been in the same families for generations, with each generation caring for them in their time and place.

MATERIALS

(for four chair pads)

- ¹/₄ yard (22.9 cm) gold for first house
- ¹/₄ yard (22.9 cm) mauve for second house
- ¹/₄ yard (22.9 cm) dark red for third house
- ¹/₄ yard (22.9 cm) teal green for fourth house
- ¹/₂ yard (45.7 cm) light blues for sky
- ¹/₂ yard (45.7 cm) dark blue for sky
- ¹/₂ yard (45.7 m) total of black and various dark tweeds or plaids for roofs
- ¹/₂ yard (45.7 cm) total of various medium, light, and dark greens for hills
- ¹/₈ yard (11.4 cm) brown for paths and rocks
- Scraps: grays for insides of windows; white or ivory, tan, dark purple, dark green for outlining houses; rust or gold for doors; black or navy for outlining

Four Coastal House Chair Pads

Each 12" x 12" (30.5 x 30.5 cm)

(Patterns, page 119)

This project includes four chair pads: a gold flattop, a mauve Nova Scotian–style house, a red pitched roof, and a teal green saltbox.

Houses are among the simplest objects to hook. Choosing colors is like painting your house—you pick a trim color and a body color and off you go. The most common mistake that people make when hooking houses is outlining the top of the roof with the trim color of the house. I like to ask them, "Do you get up on your roof and paint a line of your house trim across the top of it?"

I choose dark colors for a roof. Deep plaids or tweeds work well, producing a shingled effect. You can hook the roof in a diagonal line to enhance the slanted shape of it. Some people like to hook houses in straight, horizontal lines to create a clapboard effect.

The landscape areas in these chair pads are small, so add only small bits of accent colors to the foreground greens. If you add too much color or too many colors, the hooked pads will look patchy. The same is true of the sky, too. Choose one or two blues to use predominantly in the sky of each pad. Even though the pieces

are small, I mixed three or four shades of blue for the water because I felt that this part of the pad needed to be identifiable as water. You don't need to make the skies, water, and land the same colors in each rug. These small pieces are great for learning how you can use different colors in each area to get different effects.

Before transferring the designs to your backing, measure the seat of your chairs to see what size chair pad will fit comfortably. You can finish your chair pads with a backing of wool or velvet. To create a cushiony effect, stuff the center slightly with a row or two of quilt batting. These pads can also be tied to the chair backs if you want them to stay in place. Simply attach corner ties.

"A coastal house has to be comfortable if it is going to protect you from the elements. Some new houses built right on the water without a bit of respectful distance scare me. Having watched the water all my life, I would not want to be too close to its edge when the sea is all riled up."

MATERIALS

- $^1/_2$ yard (45.7 cm) total of various dark khaki and forest greens for back hills
- $^1/_4$ yard (22.9 cm) total of various bright and deep blues for water
- $^1/_8$ yard (11.4 cm) total of various light greens for foreground grass
- $^1/_8$ yard (11.4 cm) pale blue for first house
- $^1/_8$ yard (11.4 cm) salmon for second house
- $^1/_8$ yard (11.4 cm) brown for third house
- $^1/_8$ yard (11.4 cm) dusty blue for fourth house
- $^1/_8$ yard (11.4 cm) sage green for fifth house
- $^1/_4$ yard (22.9 cm) black for outlining
- $^1/_2$ yard (45.7 cm) total of various dark plaids for roofs
- Details: gold, white, rose, pink, teal blue, wine, and green for house trims and doors; gray for inside windows; taupes to highlight background hills

Company Houses on the Coast

72" x 18" (1.8 m x 45.5 cm)

(Pattern, page 120)

I see these sorts of rugs as "dreamscapes"—fictional places that marry some of my favorite ideas. There are several sets of rowhouses in Amherst left over from the town's industrial heyday at the turn of the century. When I am walking through the town, I love to watch the pattern that they make. From the window seat at the local tavern, you can look across the tracks to an old industrial part of town and see a row of typical Amherst houses painted in tan, aqua, red, and brown.

Hooked rugs do not need to be squares, rectangles, ovals, or circles. They can be any shape. I like to contour the shape of a rug, as I've done here, along the line of the hillside. When contouring a rug, be careful not to make the edges too jagged, or they will be difficult to bind. If your contours are soft organic shapes, instead of binding the raw edges, you can just fold the backing to the back to hide the edges. Then hand-sew the turned edge along the backside of the rug with small stitches.

This type of rug has an almost sculptural quality when hanging on a wall. The unusual shape clearly gives it a contemporary style. Accentuate the back hills by contrasting the shades of green in them. In the foreground, I accented the grass with some heavily textured shades of green. Sometimes, materials that are too thick to work with easily make great accents, making the rug almost three-dimensional.

Add a brown, gold, blue or yellow hill for extra dimension—remember, contrasting shades will make the hills stand out. Get out your tweeds and plaids for the roofs. There's a lot of roof area. Solid shades or too many dark colors will flatten out this design and make it dull. You could easily adapt this pattern by putting ladders on some of the roofs, adding a boat in the water, or having an upside-down dory in the yard. Make it your own "dreamscape."

FIELDS OF THE NORTHUMBERLAND STRAIT
diptych, each 22" x 36" (56 x 91.5 cm)

Making rugs has made me look at the world much more closely. What once was a big green field to me is now a big quilt of color and texture. I see clusters of goldenrod, the blowing timothy turning from mauve to gray, and the patches of wild rose in a new way. As I walk by the fields at the shore, I search for texture and color, striving to translate the natural sheep's wool and handspun yarns that I have into landscape. For years I had walked by these fields without really seeing them. One summer, they blossomed in my work, emerging as big tapestries of hay, flower, and earth.

"When designing rugs, I can lift a beautiful set of buildings from town and place them by the sea. It is a bit like a magical play set because I can take the best of everything and put them together as I would want them to be."

MAKING FRINGE

Every now and then, you might want to try adding fringe to a hooked rug or wall hanging. For *Road Less Traveled*, I wound burlap twine around a piece of cardstock about 5" (12.5 cm) wide. After winding it twenty times or so, I slid the strands off the card and tied one end of the wound loop tightly. I then cut the other end of the loop to create the fringe. I trimmed the ends neatly and then hand-sewed each strand of fringe to the edge of the rug. Wool yarns also make a beautiful fringe for a floor mat or wall hanging.

ROAD LESS TRAVELED
20" x 39" (51 x 99 cm)

The tassels on this rug are made of jute and trimmed with wool yarn. This is the only rug I have ever embellished with tassels.

Gold House on the Coast

28" x 16" (71 x 40.5 cm)

(Pattern, page 120)

In this rug, you can see how easy it is to use up extra bits of this and that when hooking landscape. Orange, rust, yellow, red, mauve pink, and lime strands are hooked into the hills and foreground, three or four loops at a time, to create the effect of flowers or light. A yellow house in the foreground almost always works as a design element. There seems to be something about a buttery yellow or gold that draws the viewer right into the scene.

When you are hooking rocks or cliffs, don't be afraid to slip in some color. For years I relied on grays or tans for these areas, but I now find that a mauve or pink tweed or other tweeds in soft colors add dimension to a rug.

I recently began framing some small rugs as wall hangings. Sometimes, a small piece can look lost on a wall. Putting them in a frame is like having them say, "I should be here. This is where I belong." I have the frames built to the size of the rug. Before creating the design, I lay the frame on the backing and trace the opening to be sure the design will fit within it exactly. I glue the finished piece to a Masonite backing before framing it. Choose a frame color that will appear in the piece to complement the hooked design.

MATERIALS

- $1/4$ yard (22.9 cm) total of various light blues for sky

- $1/4$ yard (22.9 cm) total of various medium to dark blues for water

- $1/2$ yard (45.7 cm) total of various greens, rusts, wines for land

- $1/8$ yard (11.4 cm) black for roof outline

- $1/8$ yard (11.4 cm) dark wine plaid for roof

- $1/8$ yard (11.4 cm) pale gold for house

- $1/8$ yard (11.4 cm) mauve for house

- Scraps: dyed natural sheep's wool for flowers; mauve tweed for rocks; dark purple and dark green for house trims; dark gray tweed for inside windows

Pitched Roofs under a Starry Sky

11" x 50" (28 cm x 1.27 m)
(Pattern, page 120)

The main component of this rug is the night sky. The houses simply lie beneath it. This type of design gives you a lot of opportunity to learn to trust your intuition as you choose from your pile of dark blues for the night sky. This is the kind of rug you can get lost in. Don't be afraid to add many different colors—this rug can handle lots of texture and motion. It would also look great with some purples or blue-greens worked in a circular motion. Notice that the reds in the sky are hooked in a truly random fashion. It's important to do the unexpected when you are making artistic rugs. Avoid being predictable!

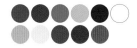

MATERIALS

- 1 yard (0.9 m) total of various navies, royal blues, and dark blue tweeds, for night sky

- $1/4$ yard (22.9 cm) total of various medium to bright lime greens for the hills

- $1/4$ yard (22.9 cm) black for roofs

- $1/8$ yard (11.4 cm) white for house outlines

- $1/8$ yard (11.4 cm) gold for house

- $1/8$ yard (11.4 cm) light blue for house

- $1/8$ yard (11.4 cm) of rust for house

- $1/8$ yard (11.4 cm) kelly green for house

- $1/8$ yard (11.4 cm) total of various reds for swirls in sky

- Scraps: yellow for inside of windows; grays for rocks and door; rust for door; blue gray tweeds, handspun yarns, and red plaids for highlights in night sky

HALF MOON NIGHT

11" x 11" (28 x 28 cm)

In rugs with a night sky, I like filling the insides of the house windows with bits of yellow or gold to show that the lights are on. Coming home at night to find the lights on is comforting. It means that someone is waiting up for you, expectant of your arrival, waiting inside with a cup of tea or a story. Imagine this rug without the illuminated windows. It would say, "We've gone to bed. See you in the morning."

MAKE ME A CHANNEL

4'8" x 5' (1.4 x 1.5 m)

When we live in a community, we need to be at peace with each other. Our houses are close together, and boundaries are not clearly defined. The only thing we know for sure is that we need to be good to one another.

Across the Fence

52" x 18" (1.32 m x 45.5 cm)

(Pattern, page 121)

When you create village-style rugs, you will want to show partial houses along with whole houses. The variety will add depth to the scene of a pictorial rug.

For this rug, I separated the larger houses in the foreground from the smaller houses in the background with a carded natural sheep's wool that had been dyed a rich brown. Natural sheep's wool in rose and green shades, approximating rose bushes, create the illusion that the houses are even farther away. Making the foreground hill higher than the door—so that it even covers parts of the windows on the white house in the foreground—was a simple but sucessful way to add depth, perspective, and dimension to the scene.

MATERIALS

- $1/2$ yard (45.7 cm) total of various greens for landscape

- $1/2$ yard (45.7 cm) total of various royal and periwinkle blues for water

- $1/4$ yard (22.9 cm) white for first house

- $1/8$ yard (11.4 cm) black-and-white tweed for roof

- $1/4$ yard (22.9 cm) black for roofs and outline

- $1/4$ yard (22.9 cm) dark gold for second house

- $1/8$ yard (11.4 cm) yellow for third house

- $1/8$ yard (11.4 cm) red plaid for fourth house

- $1/8$ yard (11.4 cm) red for fifth house

- $1/8$ yard (11.4 cm) total of coral and rust for background houses

- Scraps: plaids or tweeds for windows and small roofs; wines, red, black, and white for house trims; gray for rocks; handspun yarns and fleece for flowers; unspun brown wool for field

CHAPTER 6

Life by the Sea

This morning I took a sharp knife and cut the fins off the gray-and-cream back of a salted codfish. I bought the fish at the Halifax Farmers' Market from a Portuguese vendor a couple of weeks ago. It was the first time in years that I had seen a whole fish salted. I was taken aback by nostalgia and shelled out a hard-earned forty dollars, an astounding price for a fish. It reminded me of growing up in Freshwater where there were fish drying everywhere, hanging off the sides of sheds and lying on flakes in my next-door neighbor's front yard. At that time, we were more connected to the food we ate, especially the fish. We knew who caught it and who cured it.

I hung the fish in my studio and drew it a few dozen times, reacquainting myself with its lines and form, getting used to it again. Later, as I cut it up to soak for the following day's supper, it occurred to me how far removed from the fishery I have become in just one generation. Both my mother and my father salted the fish their fathers caught. As a child, my mother spent summers on the Labrador coast with her family, catching and salting cod to sell for the winter's provisions. My father started fishing inshore with his father in a small dory when he was twelve. Their fish was salted, dried, and sold to market, too. Fish provided both of my parents' livelihoods.

As a child, I always bought fish right off the boat at the wharf. I don't ever remember my mother buying fish in a store—it came directly from the fisherman. When we saw the boats going by the bay in front of our house, we knew they would arrive at the wharf in about ten minutes. My father and I would get in our Volkswagen and go over to pick out a fish. I'm not telling a fish story when I say the cod were larger than I was then. "Tommy cods," as my father called the smaller fish, were thrown back into the sea. Our relationship with cod is much different now. Because of overfishing, it has become an expensive delicacy.

My parents hoped I would be far removed from the fishery and that none of their daughters should worry on shore while husbands went off in boats to eke out a living. They had no romantic notions about the fishery. As soon as they could, they wanted to get away from it and its hard labor. From as early an age as I can remember, I was indoctrinated with the idea that I would go to university and get an education—so that I would never have to gut fish at the plant, or pack crab, or haul traps. That was not the life our parents wanted for us, having barely escaped it themselves. Nevertheless, for my father, the collapse of the Newfoundland cod fishery was a heartbreaking tragedy, the mismanagement of a precious resource.

As a child, I caught trout and gutted them for our dinner. When the capelin (ocean smelt) rolled in, I was always there to carry a bucket up the hill. My mother would fry the fish, and Mr. Bernie next door would dry them in the sun in his yard. Each little fish became a jerky you could chew on as you walked down the hill. I'd sometimes peek in the pot on the stove and see the head in my mother's stew peeking back up at me with milky eyes. Later I'd sit with a plate of it, sucking on the bones, dipping the last bite of potato into the broth.

I still remain connected to my family's long fishing tradition by preparing a good feed of fish. I can still pan fry a piece of cod, lightly dipped in flour, and take it off the stove at just the right time so the fish falls apart in moist flakes, with little beads of juice rolling around the edges. Fish and Brewis—a delicious Newfoundland dish of dried soaked bread and salt cod, smothered in onions and pork fat—has become my family's traditional Christmas Eve dinner, but I buy the fish flash-frozen from a factory ship. The salt cod most often comes as bits in a little plastic bag, oversalted and dingy gray, not the light rich creamy yellow that a salt fish ought to be.

I also have a link to the fishery through my rugs. I have been inspired both by my family history and by the simple shapes of the fish. I think about how they used to look laid one upon the other in my mother's white porcelain sink. I know the peach underbelly of a trout and the color of salmon flesh. Despite my connection to the fishery, one of my favorite rugs taught me how limited my knowledge really is. I had been inspired by a rug created in the early 1900s by Rhoda Dawson, a designer at the Grenfell Mission in Newfoundland. She had hooked a very detailed rug of salt fish on a flake. I decided to create a salt fish rug of my own. I drew the fish in a semigeometric fashion and hooked them in simple, light colors against an aqua background. My Uncle Donald came to visit, and I showed him the rug. He said, "Sure, they're not cod. You got the tails split— a cod's tail is not split like that." He was right, of course. The man had lived in New York for forty-five years, working on the high steel, and had not fished in more than fifty, but he knew codfish in a way that I never could. I had been saved from the fishery, yet I can't get it out of my system, no matter how many rugs I hook. After all, it's only been a generation.

WOMAN FROM THE PLANT
50" x 18" (1.3 m x 46 cm)

When I was growing up, I watched women getting dressed to go to work in the plant and later watched them returning home from it. Work at the plant was often the first job a woman had outside of raising her kids. It was hard, cold, difficult work. I remember noticing their reddened hands as they walked up the hill after finishing their shift.

School of Fish

25" x 34" (63.5 x 86.5 cm)

(Pattern, page 121)

Have fun with the fish details. Add some interesting bits of homespun yarns, natural sheep's wool, and metallic threads. When hooking the fins and eyes and adding flecks in the body, choose strong colors that stand out against the gray bodies. Outline the fish in strong colors, too. Be sure to also outline the gills, fins, and tail accents.

In the border, I hooked red in wavy lines, as if it were the sea. These wavy lines follow the curves of the shaped border. The background is hooked so the fish look like they are laid upon it, with color spread throughout each part of the area. To create this effect, be sure that you sometimes continue lines of the same color on each side of a fish. The fish will appear to float on top of the background.

Do not be afraid of strong bright colors here, because the gray and the soft blue background will really tone down the rug. If you use textured materials, such as nubby yarns, the details will stand out even more. Make the details or the eyes on each fish different—you want each one to have its own personality. I have hooked each fish in one predominant tweed but have added a similar tweed to accent the shape of the fish and to give it a little movement.

MATERIALS

- 1 yard (0.9 m) total of various reds for border
- 3/4 yard (68.6 cm) total of various medium and light blues for background
- 1/4 yard (22.9 cm) dark mauve or light purple for middle border
- 1/4 yard (22.9 cm) orange for outlining borders and fish
- 1/8 yard (11.4 cm) black for fish
- 1/2 yard (45.7 cm) total of various dark gray-green tweeds for fish
- 1/2 yard (45.7 cm) total of various light gray-green tweeds for fish
- Scraps: red and purples for outlining fish; pink, purples, royal blues, and coral handspun wools for eyes and fish details

"Our ocean once teemed with fish. As a child, I remember looking into the hole in the boat where the fisherman threw the cod and seeing the fish swirling layer upon layer on top of each other. Memory is a great resource for an artist."

MATERIALS

- ¹/₄ yard (22.9 cm) total of various reds
- ¹/₄ yard (22.9 cm) total of various dark grays
- Scraps: rose for lips, lime for outline of border, periwinkle blue for gills and eyes, and multicolored scraps of wool cloth and yarns for fish details and border

Funky Fish

12" x 24" (30.5 x 61 cm)
(Pattern, page 122)

When you choose the reds for the background, look for three types: a dark maroon red, a cherry red, and a red with some orange in it. Make sure that you use a very strong color, like the lime wool in this rug, to outline the red background behind the fish to clearly separate it from the border.

This border is truly hooked randomly, with little thought to pattern or color. That approach works well because there are similar random highlights on the fish. Make the fish lips good and thick by working with an extra-wide strip of pink material. Accentuating the lips gives the front of the fish a strong, heavy look.

There is a bit of an art to frying fish. The first few times I did, it crumbled in the pan, and I made a mess of it. When you buy fish, look for the thickest pieces that you can find. Cut these fillets into serving pieces. For 2 lbs. (0.8 kg) of fish, mix together one egg and 3/4 cup (180 ml) of milk.

Dip each piece into the milk mixture, then in the flour. Cover the bottom of a nonstick fry pan with oil. The real experts, like my mother, heat up a good cast-iron pan. Place pan over medium heat. When the oil is very hot, immediately lay the fish into the pan. The cooking times may vary, depending on the thickness of the fish, but I like to cook it on one side for about four minutes so that it is firm when I turn it over. Turn it with a spatula and cook five minutes more, lowering the heat to medium low. When you take the fish out of the pan, you want it to still have those little beads of moisture between the layers of flesh—this, I think, is where the flavor is.

I eat fried fish with vinegar. My mother used to tell me it cuts the fat. Everything written here but that is true.

This playful hulk of a fish is more reminiscent of a sculpin than any other fish I have seen. For a fish to be funky, it needs to have a certain foolishness about it. For example, this fish has purple eyes and a purple curlicue on his fin. I added some orange silk yarn to accentuate his gills and threw in a bit of yellow for some further foolishness. The lime green frame topped it all off.

MATERIALS

- $1/4$ yard (22.9 cm) ivory or cream for fish
- $1/2$ yard (45.7 cm) light gray tweed for fish
- $1/2$ yard (45.7 cm) medium gray for fish
- $1/2$ yard (45.7 cm) dark gray for fish
- $1/4$ yard (22.9 cm) total of various blacks and dark greens for border
- 1 yard (0.9 m) total of various light aqua blues
- Scraps: wines, taupe, golds, dark blues, and dark teals to outline fish and borders

Salt Cod

20" x 42" (51 cm x 1.1 m)

(Pattern, page 122)

This rug was a challenge. It required that I develop a simple but recognizable shape that could be repeated in a pattern. I also needed to be able to recall the shape of a salt codfish. Translating complicated shapes into simple, stylized ones is at the heart of creating patterns to hook. You want to get your visual ideas down to a basic set of simple lines that are easy to outline and fill in.

I created a background of pale aqua blues to approximate water. For one of the fish, I made strips from a scarf that had metallic threads in it, so that it would have a bit of a shimmer, almost as if it were wet. I looked for grays that were not too flat, but had flecks of cream or mauve in them.

I outlined the fish with playful red and yellow because to make them black would have given the rug a more geometric look than I wanted. I wanted to create the appearance of fish on a flake, which is the stand that fish are dried on. The fish bodies are in both creams and grays, so some would look as if they were skin side up while others would be flesh side up.

The thin dark border of mixed dark greens and blacks sets off the rug as if it were framed. The border is separated from the aqua background by two rows of hooking: one row of gold and one row of dark teal that almost blends in with the border color. The yellow clearly separates the border from the background, and the dark teal makes the transition to black. The colors of these lines of hooking are important choices, as they set off the central design.

This rug hangs in our little cottage on the Amherst Shore behind my hooking frame. I have kept it for myself as a gentle reminder of my forebears and what I have come from. Once the sea was an industry for my family, something that had to be bargained with for a livelihood. Now it provides a pastime, something to be watched from a comfortable distance. I think of how it must have been for my ancestors to settle such a rocky barren coast where there was barely enough soil to grow a garden.

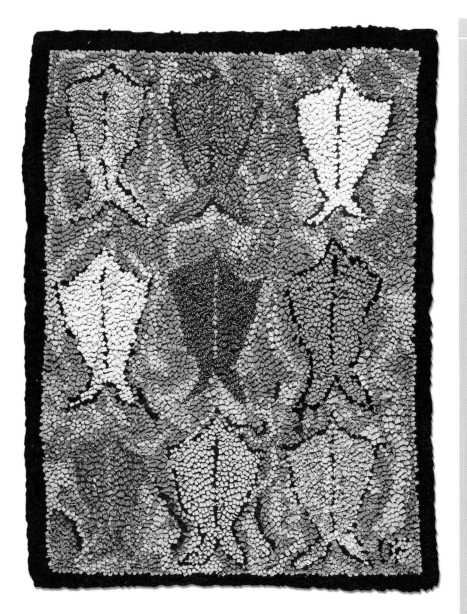

WHAT COLOR IS THE SEA?

I create water mixes of color to get a realistic effect. The secret to creating a great mix is finding colors that really sing together. I never use just one color, and I don't always rely on blue. When I look closely at really deep water, I can see that it is more green than blue. When I look at the small pond in my backyard, I discover that the water is really brown. Of course, the colors change depending on the weather and the color of the sky on any given day.

To make a great mix, you need to choose a good base color. Then add fibers in a couple of shades that are really close to it. Next, add colors that are a shade or two lighter. Sometimes, I throw in a tweed fiber that that has some of the colors I have already chosen. I will often use a fleece or textured yarn of a similar shade, too. For example, I might use three shades of marine blue, throw in a royal blue, a deep dusty blue, and a blue tweed. Then I might highlight the mix with a medium-blue fleece. Cluster the fibers to see what they look like together. If one color doesn't seem to work, remove it and add another. Rely on your intuition.

Mr. Bernie in the Cabbage Garden
48" x 30" (1.2 m x 76 cm)

Mr. Bernie and Mrs. Edna Dollimont were my well-loved neighbors when I was growing up. They treated me as if I were their grandchild, partly because all their own grandchildren were on the mainland and returned only in the summer for visits. Whenever I would catch capelin or go trouting, I would take the leftover fish guts or the extra capelin to Mr. Bernie to throw on his garden. He was a quiet, tall, thin, sort of stiff-boned man, who was as traditional a Newfoundlander as you can find.

Love across the Harbor
58" x 32" (1.5 m x 81 cm)

The two people in the border of this rug are in a struggle with one another. They see things differently and, perhaps only for a little while, they are lost to each other.

WATCHING THE BOAT

38" x 32" (96.5 x 81.5 cm)

Atlantic Canadians have an affection for
boats and lighthouses because for centuries
we have depended on them. That love has
endured, not only because these things are
part of our cultural identity, but also because
they are beautiful. They make us believe in
ourselves, acknowledging who we are and
what we came from.

Dory at the Fish Shack

34" x 10" (86.5 x 25.5 cm)

(Pattern, page 122)

Fish shacks or "stores" are where fishermen fix and store their nets, traps, and other equipment. I recently discovered that the fishing shack is also the place where fishermen gather on Saturday nights. Cruising around the harbor, you can peek in the well-lit windows of the stores and see small groups of three or four men standing around talking, with beer bottles in hand. It's no surprise, then, on a Sunday morning, to find the women on the wharf, working away, driving the fork lifts, and loading the fish onto the trucks.

Small details, like the diamond-shaped window, add a sense of place to this rug. It makes the shack look as if it belongs to someone. When you want to shape a rug, sometimes you can follow the natural shape of the subject matter. For this rug, I followed the roof line of the shack and the shape of the hills. A small, shaped rug like this one fits well over doors and windows, and sometimes can even serve as the window treatment.

When selecting dark greens for the back hills, try to get some dark blue greens to hook in with the other greens. These shades will pick up the blue of the water and unify the rug. When you hook natural sheep's wool, hook it high. I bring it up through the backing almost 1" (2.5 cm). When I hook the next loop, the first loop is pulled back down to ½" (1.3 cm). Don't be afraid of the wool—you own it, so use it as you want to.

MATERIALS

- ¼ yard (22.9 cm) total of various bright to medium blues and mauves

- ⅛ yard (11.4 cm) total of various dark and lighter greens for landscape and dory trim

- ⅛ yard (11.4 cm) deep rust for shack

- ⅛ yard (11.4 cm) gold

- ⅛ yard (11.4 cm) gray and tan tweed for roof

- Scraps: white for shack trim; black for outline and inside windows; brown tweed for rocks and cliffs; pale yellow for door; pinks, yellows, corals, and purple sheep's wool for flowers

WORKERS FROM THE PLANT

39" x 14" (99 x 35.5 cm)

I knew from the time I was a child that I did not want to work at the fish plant. The cold, wet job of cutting and splitting fish after fish, while standing on a cement floor all day, was too much for me. I saw the drawn tired faces of the workers returning from the plant each day. The women wore hairnets with little white plastic tiaras and red-tipped black rubber boots and carried their big knives by their sides as they walked up over the hill.

The Potato Pickers
7' x 3' (2.1 x 0.9 m)

This rug is about women's work and motherhood. On the coast you can see weather approaching, as these women do. They know those potatoes need to get in before the storm arrives. They are no doubt thinking about where their children are and whether their husbands are in off the boat. I love the strength shown in the curve of the woman's shoulders as she lifts the heavy tin bucket of potatoes to take them into her cellar. The shoulders of a good woman can bear a great deal.

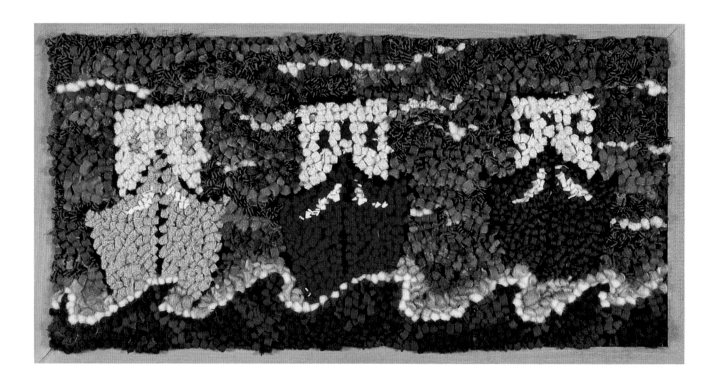

MATERIALS

- $1/4$ yard (22.9 cm) total of various very dark blues for bottom wave

- $1/8$ yard (11.4 cm) white for waves and boat tops

- $1/8$ yard (11.4 cm) gold for boat

- $1/8$ yard (11.4 cm) red for boat

- $1/8$ yard (11.4 cm) dark green for boat

- $1/2$ yard (45.7 cm) total of various medium to dark blues solids and tweeds

- Scraps: textured yarn for tops of waves, black or navy for outlining

Three for Shore
23" x 11" (58.5 x 28 cm)
(Pattern, page 123)

When hooking the background, remember to hook the water as if it were continuous behind the boats—in other words, you should hook the blues on one side of the boat and on the other side of the boat, too. To create the appearance of water, the color needs to flow in a continuous shape.

The line of black down the center front of each boat and the bits of white highlight on the hulls make the boats appear as if they are coming toward you. The heavy, deep blue wave in the foreground makes this rug more decorative than pictorial. The boats appear to be riding the big wave. The lines of white in the water approximate waves and create a bit of perspective.

GROWN UP AROUND THE COAST
54" x 22" (1.4 m x 56 cm)

Highly textured wools, such as bouclé, natural sheep's wool, roving, and handspun yarns, can create a three-dimensional garden within a traditional village landscape. Simply hook these materials as if you were hooking a strip of cloth, pulling the loops nice and high so you create the heavy texture of a full, rich landscape.

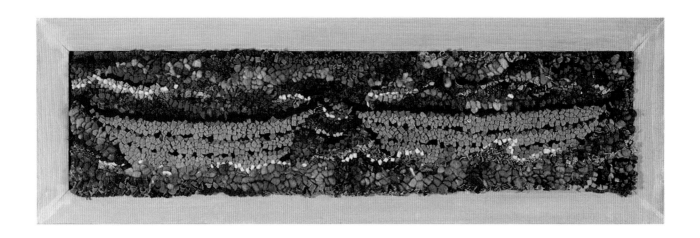

MATERIALS

- $3/4$ yard (68.6 cm) total of various blues for water

- $1/4$ yard (22.9 cm) gold for dories

- Scraps: dark green for outlining dories, white for waves, blue yarns and natural sheep's wool for water highlights

Two Golden Dories

35" x 9" (89 x 23 cm)

(Pattern, page 123)

At one time, the painted dory was a staple of the inshore fishery in Atlantic Canada. Now it is a cultural symbol, an icon left over from the days when groups of men rowed out to the fishing grounds to haul herring in nets. There are plenty of old stories of babies being born in dories, too. The truth is, I have never actually sat in a dory, and neither have most people who live here. These traditional boats are no longer easy to find.

To add interest, I accentuated the waves with a line of white right where the dories meet the water. The line is different on each dory, just as it would be if the boats were actually in the water.

There are many shades of blue in this water, from pale gray blue to deep teal blue, but most of it is hooked in a medium blue with a hint of royal blue. I highlighted the green outline of the dories with a darker gold. I also drew the lines on the side of the dories with dark green. A traditional dory does not have green stripes, but there are shadows along the sides because of the way the wooden boards overlap. The outline creates the look of the indentations.

Sometimes in primitive-style rug hooking, you cannot show things as they actually are because you are limited by the width of your materials and your selection of colors. In these cases, you have to find the best way to get the effect you are looking for, without trying to make the elements realistic.

Coastal Schooner

36" x 24" (91.5 x 61 cm)

(Pattern, page 123)

When you hook water, work with many different shades of blue. Start by hooking waves all over as a guide and then hook in the other colors. In this rug, there are nine shades of blue: a light mauve, a teal-and-white tweed, a dark teal, a gray blue, a dusty blue tweed, a dusty blue, an aqua blue, a navy blue, and a royal blue.

It's important to hook the water in wavy lines if you want to show movement. Be careful not to stripe the colors. In some areas, work the same colors several times to create small bodies of color. In other areas, hook long, wavy sinews. Alternate these two styles throughout the water area.

The sails should look as if they are blowing a bit. You can create this effect by highlighting the creamy areas with a bright, white wool. White wool is hard to find. Wool comes off the sheep as a natural cream color, so the lightest shades of cream are as close to a natural white as you'll get. For the sails, you can soak some cream wool in a bath of tea for several hours to give the wool a soft, tan color.

MATERIALS

- $3/4$ yard (68.6 cm) total of white and various creams for flowers, outlining, and sails

- $1/4$ yard (22.9 cm) black for boat hull

- $1/4$ yard (22.9 cm) total of various tans and gold for flower centers, boat details, and scrolls

- $3/4$ yard (68.6 cm) total of various blues for water

- $3/4$ yard (68.6 cm) very dark and medium wine

- Scraps: pale mauve for water highlights

"My Uncle Donald, who is one of the least romantic people I know, told me that he was so anxious to leave the outport where he grew up that, as soon as he was old enough, he 'jumped aboard the first schooner that came in the harbor.'"

RAISIN BUNS

My mother made these raisin buns three or four times a week because having them around meant she always had something to serve someone with a cup of tea. They are a simple baking-powder biscuit made with a dark raisin.

2 cups (250 g) flour
3 teaspoons (15 g) baking powder
1/4 cup (50 g) sugar
1/2 teaspoon salt
1/2 cup (112 g) butter
1 egg
3/4 cup (175 ml) milk
3/4 cup (50 g) dark raisins

Blend the dry ingredients. Cut in butter until you have a coarse meal. Mix in the raisins. Add the egg and milk, stirring until you have a heavy, but not-too-sticky dough. Roll the dough out on a floured surface to 1" (2.5 cm) thickness. Cut the dough into circles with a drinking glass. Bake in a preheated 400°F (200°C) oven for 12 to 15 minutes. Serve with butter.

WRAPPED IN A QUILT
18" x 34" (45.5 x 86.5 cm)

I love the chill of a summer night after a warm day. Wrapping yourself in the comfort of a quilt is such a gift.

WOMAN IN BLUE DRESS
30" x 50" (76 cm x 1.3 m)

Real beauty is about being comfortable with yourself. This woman knows all about it and can hold an entire room captive.

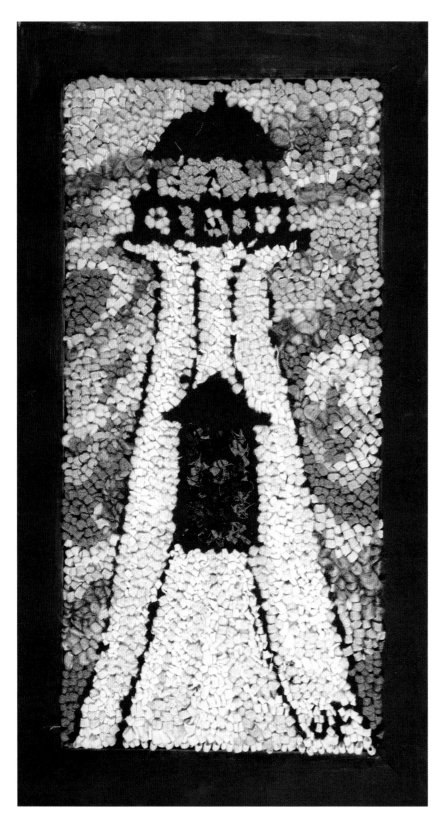

Peak of the Light

11" x 23" (28 x 58.5 cm)

(Pattern, page 124)

The background of this rug could be hooked in light blues, as shown here, to create the appearance of sky, or in deeper, dustier blues to create water. To emphasize the length of the peak and to make it look like the viewer is looking up at the light, hook the whites and creams in horizontal lines on a slight slant.

I hooked the windowpanes in dark gray, the color they actually are when you are looking in from the outside. It might be tempting to hook the panes in yellow to further illuminate the house, but this might detract from the peak of the lighthouse. It is important to create a focal point in your rug. If you have too many things going on, the elements in the finished piece will compete with each other.

MATERIALS

- ⅛ yard (11.4 cm) red for trim

- ½ yard (45.7 cm) total of various whites for house

- ½ yard (45.7 cm) total of various pale light blues for sky

- Scraps: gray tweeds for inside windows, gold and yellow for light

SKINNY-DIPPING NEAR THE ISLANDS
38" x 16" (96.5 x 40.5 cm)

Sometimes in rugs I do things that I would love to do in real life, but probably won't. For example, I won't be jumping off a dory into the Atlantic in the buff on a sunny afternoon for a swim—but I'd like to think I might.

"Anyone who has ever been on a rough sea knows that the lighthouse is a beacon. It is a symbol of being led toward home, of being cared for, and guided safely. People remember being guided ashore by the lights or of hearing their father talk of the time he was 'so glad to see the light.'"

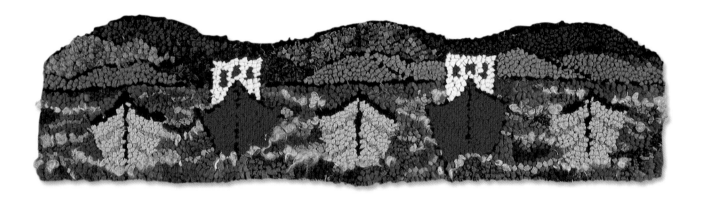

Cape Islanders and Dories Coming Ashore

40" x 9" (1 m x 23 cm)
(Pattern, page 124)

MATERIALS

- $1/4$ yard (22.9 cm) total of various greens for hills
- $1/2$ yard (45.7 cm) total of various blues for water
- $1/8$ yard (11.4 cm) gold for dories
- $1/8$ yard (11.4 cm) red for Cape Islanders
- $1/8$ yard (11.4 cm) white for boat tops
- Scraps: tan for dory and hill highlights; gray natural sheep's wool for waves

Picture yourself on the back of a boat, watching how the rush of the boat toward the shore is creating so much activity in the water. The water near the edges of the boat will be thick and foamy. Hook the waves high and thick before you hook the water around them.

The shape of this hooked piece—which makes a good door or window topper—is defined by the hills themselves. I outlined the hills in black to make them distinct and to get that "rolling" feeling. Notice how freely I mixed the blue greens and khakis together. At first, you might think that brown-based greens and blue-based greens don't match, but in nature, they coexist beautifully.

I worked with many different greens, hooking them in each hill. The idea that you need to use dark colors in the background and lighter colors in the foreground is just a general guideline, not a hard-and-fast rule. If you look closely at the hills, you will sometimes see lighter colors in the background.

The Cape Islander has been the predominant boat style in the inshore fishery since the early 1900s. In 1905, it was redesigned from a power yacht and converted to a motorized fishing boat. Initially, these boats were built from wood, but since the 1970s they have been made of fiberglass, which lasts longer and requires less maintenance. The versatile Cape Islander serves as both lobster boat and scallop dragger and is used for long lining (commercial fishing) and sport fishing. In recent years, as fish stocks have declined, boat builders have merged the Cape Islander's practical past with a new role, creating a "lobster yacht," an elegant cruising vessel for wealthy passengers.

Standing before the Monument
8' x 6' (2.4 x 1.8 m)

The border of this rug says, "Unlike the poet, my life has most often taken the road well travelled and I have made it whole with gifts of bread to neighbors." I believe our lives are made complete by the small beauties of the everyday, rather than by grand plans.

CHAPTER 7

When All the Women Wore Dresses

My mother's perfume was Javex. It is a fragrance that I still associate with her, the fragrance of whiteness, of hard wrinkled hands with knuckles too large for their fingers. My mother was a hard worker, but she was not the only one working her fingers to the bone. Most of the women in our community were cleaning house, cleaning fish, or, like my mother, cleaning the ferry boats.

On Tuesday and Saturday nights, after the housework was done, my mother and her friends, Mrs. Kitty and Mrs. Edna, would walk down to the parish hall for bingo. Their dress was typical of the period. My mother, the youngest and most modern of the group, often wore polyester elastic-waist slacks in navy or dark brown. The other women wore dresses that showed beneath their calf-length camel-hair coats. All three would have spent the day before wearing curlers in their hair, covered by bandanas that were tied in the back. At night, with their fresh hairdos, they put on fresh bandanas, tied beneath the chin, to protect their hair from the fog and wind as they wandered down the path to bingo. Each woman wore the same coat year after year, freshening it with a new bandana (and recycling last year's as the daytime curler hold). My mother wore bandanas until she died in April 2000—as I like to say, she brought bandanas into the new millennium. I still have the last one she wore.

During those days in the 1970s, relatively few women worked outside the home. Those who did were mostly schoolteachers. My mother, apart from her part-time summer job, stayed around the house. I was used to having her waiting for me when I came down the stairs in the morning and came home after school. Some mornings, I found her on her hands and knees sopping up water from the floor, the result of a leaking basement in the house my father had built at the base of a steep hill. As with many of my father's follies, my mother was left mopping up after him. It was her role as a woman at that time, in that place. He would spend half his time providing a paycheck for her to keep the house and pay the bills, but otherwise he was free to do as he wished. It was the way of that time, and the lives of most of her friends were the same.

COASTAL GIRLS
20" x 34" (51 x 86.5 cm)

There is great joy in being together with friends. This rug celebrates the joy we find in each other.

SCRUBBING THE FLOOR
27" x 50" (68.5 cm x 1.3 m)

This is a portrait of my mother, but I believe it is also a portrait of all mothers in working-class families.

My mother kept my life as stable and orderly as she could. She kept a warm and inviting house, with homemade bread always ready. Her role was clearly defined by her own experience, by those women around her, and, of course, by the expectations of the men they had all married. There have been times when I've looked at my mother's life as "small" and wondered if she were happy. She stayed with my father all her life and cared for him lovingly, even though she sometimes thought him to be foolish. She had a lot of good friends because she refused to be a gossip. She generally spoke well of others. When things were dark, she laughed her way toward happiness, surrounded by women who were in the same boat. Her life was not small. It was simple in many of the same ways my own life is simple.

MATERIALS

- 1/2 yard (45.7 cm) mauve for house

- 1/2 yard (45.7 cm) total of various medium to dark greens for landscape, vines, and leaves

- 1/4 yard (22.9 cm) total of various sky blues

- 1/4 yard (22.9 cm) total of various ocean blues

- 1/8 yard (11.4 cm) total of various burgundies and wines for coat and flowers

- 1/8 yard (11.4 cm) white for fence

- 1/8 yard (11.4 cm) total of various reds and oranges for flowers, scarf, and dress

- 1/4 yard (22.9 cm) black tweed or plaid for roof

- 1/4 yard (22.9 cm) black for outlining

- 1 yard (0.9 m) total of various tans for border

- Scraps: gray-green tweed for inside windows, gray for rocks, blue for flowers, dark blue for house trim

Woman on the Path

22" x 34" (56 x 86.5 cm)

(Pattern, page 124)

Look for a little light mauve to highlight the sky. This sky was hooked with a single piece of dyed wool cloth. The wool was white. I overdyed it light blue, working in a small pot of dye, so that when the wool was squashed into it, some of the white would remain. I then spot-dyed it with a little mauve. When spot dying, you add the dye randomly throughout the cloth.

Look for printed materials, such as plaids and tweeds, for the scarf and dress. These are small areas of the rug, but they're important details. I made the scarf with a variegated wool yarn. I hooked small spots of blue in the dress to create a print effect, as if the dress were calico. You might also want to show a bit of the dress color peeking out the sleeve of her coat.

The insides of the windows were made with a tweed fabric that has red and green in it. A tweed with color creates the impression of something outside reflected in the glass—or of something happening inside the house that the viewer is not a part of.

Hook the red flowers in the border with four to six different shades to give them that primitive style. Outline them in one shade, fill in with the others. Highlight the center with the brightest shade. Adding a tiny bit of gold, orange, or another bright color in the center really sets off the rest of the flower. For the woman's coat, work with two shades of burgundy—one predominant shade with a much smaller amount of the second shade—to create the effect of folds in the fabric. Make sure the blue of the sea is peeking through the palings on the fence to give this simple design more depth. Notice that there is a tiny bit of blue hooked into the grass. Just these few loops of color suggest a few, scattered forget-me-nots, while also picking up on the blue flowers in the border.

I like the idea of footpaths, the kind that are not big enough for cars or four-wheelers, just for a little walk to the neighbor's house or into the woods or down to the beach—a true "footpath." The woman in this rug has a lot of personality, not only because of her orange dress and scarf, but also because of the purple house that she is standing in front of so proudly. In any community, a purple house is noticed.

Materials

- 1/4 yard (22.9 cm) black for outlining, border, and dress

- 1 yard (0.9 m) total of various whites, creams, light grays, mauves, and other pale colors

- 1/8 yard (11.4 cm) total of various tans for skin tones

- 1/8 yard (11.4 cm) total of various teal greens for dresses

- 1/8 yard (11.4 cm) red and wine for border and outline of dresses

- 1/8 yard (11.4 cm) total of various pale and medium blues

- 1/8 yard (11.4 cm) gold for dresses

- 1/8 yard (11.4 cm) mauve for dresses

- Scraps: dyed natural sheep's wool for hair, colors to show folds in clothing, brown for purse

Dancing Women

54" x 12" (1.4 m x 30.5 cm)
(Pattern, page 125)

Hook curlicues and swirls into the background to emphasize the movement of the women and to create a bit of a partylike scene. The best way to work this is to hook the swirls in first with one of the most distinct colors. Then hook the other colors, following the swirling motion wherever you can. Remember, don't place swirls everywhere—if you do, the background will look more like a vortex that is swallowing up the women! You want the effect to be playful.

When I drew this rug, I drew the women as nudes, adding their clothing later. This process allowed me to dress them according to their body shape. As you hook the dresses, remember that clothing has folds in it, so it's important to add a little bit of a secondary color to emphasize the folds. Add flowers to any of the dresses by simply hooking in a contrasting second color and accenting that color with a bit of green. While hooking the natural sheep's wool, I made the loops high to show the wildness of the hair.

FERRY CLEANERS
52" x 38" (1.3 x 0.96 m)

This is the way I remember women when I was growing up during the 1970s. Dresses peeked out from under wool-cloth coats or raglan sweaters, and bandanas were tied under chins. My mother cleaned the ferry that carried passengers from Newfoundland to the mainland of Canada. At the end of her shift, she would eat her lunch on the boat. I would wait at the top of the hill for her to come home because she would bring me a pat of real butter to spread on a piece of toast.
Real butter was something that we would only get once a year when it was made locally.

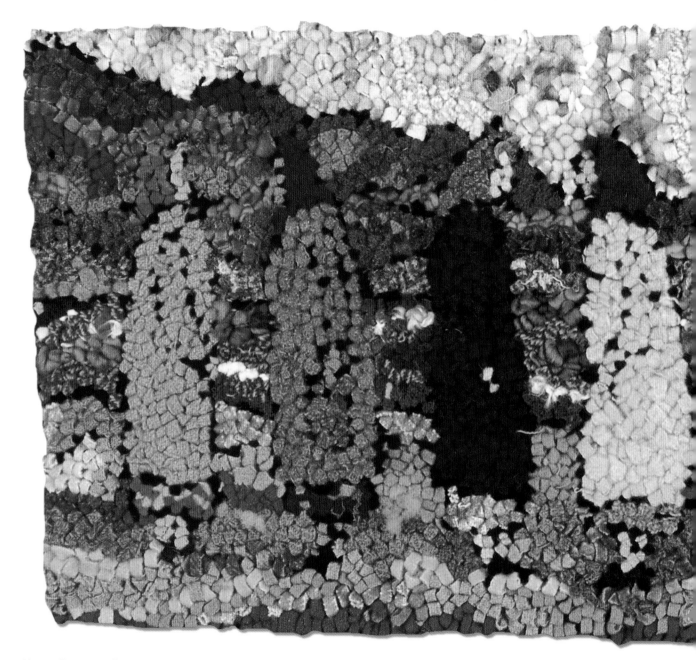

Up and Down the Coast
12" x 30" (30.5 x 76 cm)

It amazes me how news travels so fast in any small town. Once I went back home and, by the time I made my way to visit an old neighbor, three people had already told him that I was in town. I said, "Well it's a good thing I dropped in then, isn't it?" Not much gets by anyone in a small place. People know who you are before you are introduced because they have seen you from their window and asked their neighbor about you.

This rug illustrates how news flies through a town. The idea is not about gossip, although no doubt in every town there is some of that. It is about knowing everyone and passing along the facts. This piece is a parody, really, because news not only travels through the women of the community, but also through the men of the community—that will be the theme of another rug!

CHAPTER 8

The Hit-and-Miss Tradition

My mother quit rug hooking for sixty years, wanting nothing to do with it after she left her childhood home. When I began hooking rugs, she slowly came around to it again. In the last eight years of her life, she made about twenty hooked mats, giving one to each daughter and to some of her grandchildren. She would call me and say, "Now, Deanne, I wants you to mark off a mat and bring it out to me." To "mark off" the mat meant to draw it on the burlap backing.

No matter what I drew on the backing for her to make, she would find a way to put in the hit-and-miss stripes of her childhood. It was how she remembered hooking rugs. As a little girl of eight or nine, she would hook on her mother's mat after school in the front hall of their green clapboard flattop house near Brigus, Newfoundland. The striped, geometric-style hit-and-miss mat was very common in Newfoundland. As Cynthia Boyd explained in an article in *PieceWork Magazine* (January/February 1998), "What distinguishes the traditional hooked mats of Newfoundland and Labrador is the maker's attention to repetition and symmetry. Each side of the mat is subdivided in diamonds, squares, hearts, or flowers."

I find it compelling that my mother still felt the need to carry on the tradition of hit-and-miss that had been ingrained in her. I like hit-and-miss both because of my mother's affinity for it and because it is traditional. It is also a very functional way of hooking because it allows you to use up your scraps and leftover bits of fabric. In the days before you could easily buy a secondhand skirt to tear apart, scraps of fabric were precious commodities, and rug hookers created designs to use them up. I keep a basket behind my hooking chair, full of lost strips. Hit-and-miss is a kind of "stream of consciousness" hooking. You pull out random colors and hook them one after another. The lines can be perfectly straight, slightly crooked, or "higgledy piggledy"—all over the place in any direction.

Bright reds and yellows give mats an old-fashioned style, as for the posy rugs on pages 104–106 and 112. Subdued golds, rusts, and burnt reds create an antique feeling, as in the *Wavy Flower Pot* rug on page 109 and the *Traditional Six Square Atlantic Canadian Sampler* on page 107.

To me, old-fashioned is different from antique. When I say old-fashioned, I am thinking of the type of rugs that were being made by my friends' mothers in the late 1960s and early 1970s. Any color they had on hand would do—the process was truly hit and miss. In antique designs, color is more of a consideration. The dull rusts, oranges, khakis, gold, and wines reflect the colors of the natural dyes that were available to rug hookers more than 100 years ago. For these designs, you should avoid the bright commercial colors that became available later on. Work with scraps for all elements of these hit-and-miss rug designs, except for the backgrounds.

THE HOOK-IN
36" x 18" (91.5 x 45.5 cm)

Gathering together to hook rugs is a Maritimes tradition. Women pack up their wool and lap frames and gather at community halls and in one another's houses to talk, drink tea, and hook rugs. Unlike a quilting bee, where each person works on a communal quilt, at the hook-in, everyone is working on individual projects, while sharing ideas and thoughts about each other's work.

Yellow Posy Square Pad

10" x 19" (25.5 x 48.5 cm)

(Pattern, page 125)

MATERIALS

- $1/4$ yard (22.9 cm) black for background

- $1/8$ yard (11.4 cm) yellow for flower

- $1/8$ yard (11.4 cm) green for outline

- Scraps: a variety of colors for border

Nine Posies Hit-and-Miss

16" x 32" (40.5 x 81.5 cm)

(Pattern, page 126)

MATERIALS

- ³⁄₄ yard (68.6 cm) black for background
- ¹⁄₄ yard (22.9 cm) gold for flowers and outlining
- ¹⁄₄ yard (22.9 cm) red for flowers and outlining
- ¹⁄₂ yard (45.7 cm) scraps of many colors

HIT-AND-MISS HOOKING

This traditional style of hooking—called hit-and-miss—relies heavily on the direction of your hooked line. You can entirely change the way the rug looks simply by changing the direction of the hooking. You can hook this type of rug design vertically, horizontally, in curves, or on a diagonal. You can also hook "higgledy piggledy," which means that you hook in no particular direction at all, but in randomly arranged curved and straight lines. This creative method of hooking is a lot of fun and very expressive. It also provides a great way to experiment with color combinations.

MATERIALS

- $1/2$ yard (45.7 cm) total of various scraps for border and flowers

- $1/8$ yard (11.4 cm) of tan and tan tweed for outlining, flower pot, vines, and border outline

- $3/4$ yard (68.6 cm) black for background

- $1/4$ yard (22.9 cm) total of various reds and rusts for large flowers

- $1/8$ yard (11.4 cm) light green tweeds for leaves

Posy Pot Hit-and-Miss

48" x 10" (1.2 m x 25.5 cm)

(Pattern, page 126)

This mat features bold, primitive-style flower motifs. Outline them in one color, and select two or three—sometimes four or five colors—to fill in each one. Think of each flower as if it's a little work of art, just as you would if it were growing in your garden.

"Through your choice of colors and by softening the lines a bit, you can easily give traditional patterns a modern twist."

Traditional Six Square Atlantic Canadian Sampler

34" x 22" (86.5 x 56 cm)
(Pattern, page 126)

MATERIALS

- 1 yard (0.9 m) black for borders
- 1/2 yard (45.7 cm) burnt red for background
- 1/4 yard (22.9 cm) rich bright olive green for outlining
- Scraps of golds, rusts, greens, and taupe

"As you hook rugs, save all the little leftover bits in a basket. Any piece of wool longer than 4" (10 cm) is worth saving and will work well in a hit-and-miss border."

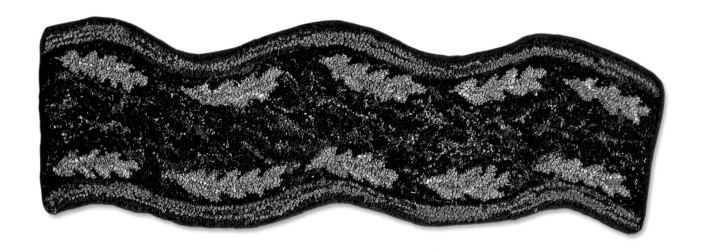

MATERIALS

- ³/₄ yard (68.6 cm) black-and-red tweed
- ³/₄ yard (68.6 cm) black
- ¹/₈ yard (11.4 cm) sage green for outlining
- ¹/₄ yard (22.9 cm) terra cotta solids and plaids for oak leaves
- ¹/₂ yard (45.7 cm) total of various scraps in greens, browns, rusts, and golds

Wavy Oak Leaves

52" x 14" (1.3 m x 35.5 cm)
(Pattern, page 127)

Somebody once told me that the oak leaf is a symbol of strength, longevity, and endurance. I think it is a wonderful symbol to use in hooked mats, which are also known for the same qualities. I have been using it ever since.

This background is a mixture of blacks and black-and-red tweed, hooked in a random pattern. I alternated colors once in a while to create a random effect throughout the background. The sides are highlighted with selected hit-and-miss scraps. Rather than pull in colors randomly, I chose colors for the hit-and-miss portion of the rug that I knew would enhance it. I wanted to keep the dark, strong feeling that I had created in the body of the rug.

The soft border curves of this rug lend a contemporary feeling to a very traditional design. I like to keep the curves soft so that the rug will lie flat. Bind the rug with black cotton twill tape, the most common style of binding found on antique mats. Binding is a practical way of preventing the edges of your floor mat from becoming frayed (page 24).

Wavy Oak Leaves and *Wavy Flower Pot* (facing page) are antique designs with a modern twist. They look great on either the floor or the wall. I like to push the boundaries of rug hooking, mixing up the traditional with the very new, to leave my mark on it.

Wavy Flower Pot

20" x 70" (51 cm x 1.8 m)

(Pattern, page 127)

Be playful when working with color. Remember, these flowers are not real. Real flowers could never emerge from a pot like this! Paint them up any way you like. You can include intensely bright colors in floor mats, but use them carefully— they can throw a rug design off balance. Be sure to decorate the pot with a bit of shape and color, as the eye will follow the vine back down to it.

I made this rug for my back door, and it has served me well. Nontraditional shapes are interesting to have on the floor. The curves on this rug are very gentle, so you'll have no trouble getting it to lie flat. The curved stripes of the border emphasize the shape of the rug. Notice the top and bottom of the rug are slanted to produce both angles and curves. The flowers emerge from the pot as if they were a vine, dancing along with the curvy shape of the rug. The blue-green vine stands out well against the mixed black background and the coral-colored pot

When you design a pot of flowers for a mat, it is important to see the pot as a complete object—just as the potter would. Plan its design and placement carefully. To focus the viewer's attention, decorate the pot with one shape or several. Try diamonds, stripes, squares, or circles. Or include a more organic design, such as a flower or leaf.

MATERIALS

- 2 yards (1.8 m) total of black and black tweeds

- $1/3$ yard (30.5 m) of light green for outlining leaves and vines

- $1/2$ yard (45.7 cm) medium blue green for leaves

- $1 1/2$ yards (1.4 m) total of various tans and brown for hit-and-miss border and vine

- $1/8$ yard (11.4 cm) total of various reds and roses for flowers and border outline

- Scraps: orange, gold, tan tweed, mauve, and burgundy tweed for leaves and flowers

Something in Common
34" x 70" (86.5 cm x 1.8 m)

One morning, in church, I saw a fourteen-year-old boy rub his mother's back. The woman had just been diagnosed with breast cancer. As I walked home, I decided that I would create a rug from various wools collected from women who had survived breast cancer. I first called my Aunt Nell on Long Island, New York, who sent me a cream shawl. I also called friends, rug hookers, and neighbors. Seventy-seven women sent me wool, and I worked with the fiber just as it came. The rug, depicting women of all ages, belongs to all the women who took part in the project. I donated it to the permanent collection of the Art Gallery of Nova Scotia. Sales of a postcard with the image raised approximately $1,000 for the Canadian Cancer Society. I donated another large rug to the Women's Cancer Program at the Mayo Clinic in Minnesota, to thank the American women who participated in the project and who have supported my work through the years. This rug celebrates life and the things we share in common.

Mermaids at Midnight

54" x 18" (1.4 m x 45.5 cm)

(Pattern, page 127)

For the mermaids "outfits," choose gaudy tweeds that will stand out against the dark colors of the midnight sea. Outline them with bright, contrasting colors. As always, when hooking people, even imaginary ones, use natural sheep's wool for hair. Choose various shades of tans, browns, taupes, and peaches to reflect different skin types. I added tiny bits of metallic thread to the mermaids' waists to approximate belt buckles, and, in one case, to ears as earrings. Be careful not to overdo the metallics.

Each mermaid is unique in form and dress. Show movement by putting their hands and arms in different positions or by tipping their tails a little. I did not outline their arms because the skin color is so distinct from the background blues that I did not need to. This way, the arms also appear slightly more delicate. The background mixes ultramarine blue, royals, and navies with jade greens for an underwater-algae effect.

These girls are out on the town and there is no stopping them. They seem to be a little like my sisters. I love the legends of fishermen who have been at sea too long, who spot mermaids only to later find them to be "truly independent" women. Imagine them in bunches! Hang onto the side of the boat, by's!

MATERIALS

- 1 1/2 yards (1.4 m) dark royal and navy blues for background
- 1/8 yard (11.4 cm) total of various tans for skin tones
- 1/8 yard (11.4 cm) purple plaid for outfits
- 1/8 yard (11.4 cm) red plaid for outfit
- 1/8 yard (11.4 cm) orange plaid for outfit
- 1/8 yard (11.4 cm) pink plaid for outfit
- 1/8 yard (11.4 cm) light blue plaid for outfit
- Scraps: textured wools or natural sheep's wool for hair, metallic threads for outfit details, bright colors for outlining outfits

MATERIALS

- 1 yard (0.9 m) light blues and mauve for background

- 1/8 yard (11.4 cm) dark purple for outlining

- 3/4 yard (68.6 cm) dark navy and royal blues for border

- 1/4 yard (22.9 cm) lime green for leaves

- 1/4 yard (22.9 cm) kelly green for leaves

- 1/2 yard (45.7 cm) total of various reds and red tweeds for flowers

- 1/3 yard (30.5 cm) dark teal for pot

- Scraps: purple, green, red, and gold for lines around border; blue sheep's wool for background highlights

Rosy Posy Pot

34" x 20" (86 x 51 cm)
(Pattern, page 127)

To give the flowers a three-dimensional look, hook the centers of the roses so the loops are slightly higher than the rest. I hooked a few swirls in the background, but mostly I tried to hook wavy lines in many different directions. I added interest to the background by hooking in some blue natural sheep's wool and a few bits of mauve, to pick up on the purple outline of the roses. The border is hooked randomly, with royal blue lightening up the dark navy.

In this style of rug, old meets new. This design is about as traditional as you can get, but the roses have a "folksier" quality than many traditional patterns. The color is also contemporary. The lime and kelly greens are intense, modern colors. The bold colors along the edge between the body and the border of green, red, and yellow also give the rug a playful appeal. The border is a mixture of dark navy and royal blues. Navy is the traditional color, and the royal blue livens it up.

EMMA IN THE CABBAGE GARDEN
22" x 54" (0.6 x 1.4 m)

This is a portrait of a grandmother who, although I never met her, has had a great influence on my life. My father's mother, Emma Wakeham Fitzpatrick, was a rug hooker. She created her own designs, filled her house with rugs, and drew patterns for many of her neighbors.

BERRY PICKING ON THE COAST
17" x 48" (43 cm x 1.2 m)

I picked blueberries as a child. My father would drive me and my mother out to the country and drop us off on the side of the road to pick the berries. He would come back two hours later to get us—and our full pails.

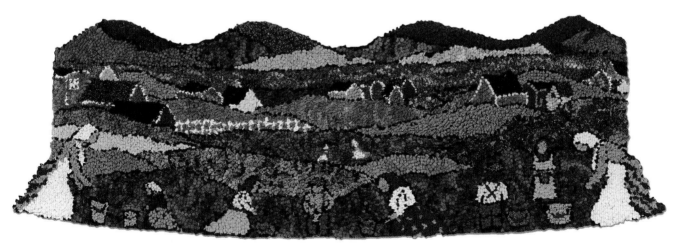

Patterns

LIVING ON THE EDGE
Page 34

WISH UPON A STARFISH
Page 35

MOOSE WELCOME
Page 36

SEASHELL WELCOME

Page 39

KISSING FISH WELCOME

Page 40

OLD-TIME LEAVES IN THE BORDER

Page 51

OLD-TIME SCROLLS
Page 52

OLD ROSE OVAL
Page 56

ANTIQUE LEAF RUNNER

Page 57

**FOUR COASTAL HOUSE
CHAIR PADS**

Page 60

COMPANY HOUSES ON THE COAST

Page 62

GOLD HOUSE ON THE COAST

Page 65

**PITCHED ROOFS UNDER
A STARRY SKY**

Page 66

ACROSS THE FENCE

Page 69

SCHOOL OF FISH

Page 73

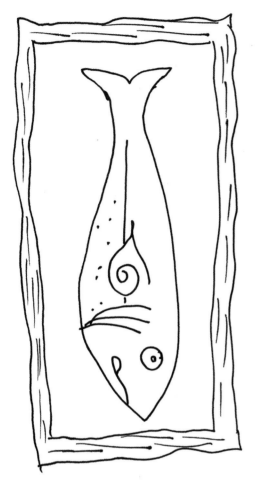

FUNKY FISH

Page 74

SALT COD

Page 76

DORY AT THE FISH SHACK

Page 81

THREE FOR SHORE

Page 84

TWO GOLDEN DORIES

Page 86

COASTAL SCHOONER

Page 87

CAPE ISLANDERS AND DORIES COMING ASHORE

Page 92

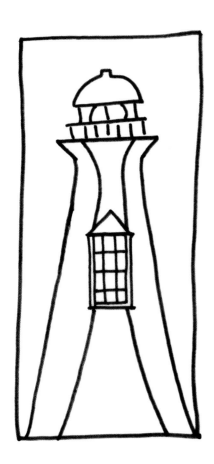

PEAK OF THE LIGHT

Page 90

WOMAN ON THE PATH

Page 96

DANCING WOMEN

Page 98

YELLOW POSY SQUARE

Page 104

NINE POSIES HIT-AND-MISS
Page 105

POSY POT HIT-AND-MISS
Page 106

TRADITIONAL SIX SQUARE
ATLANTIC CANADIAN SAMPLER
Page 107

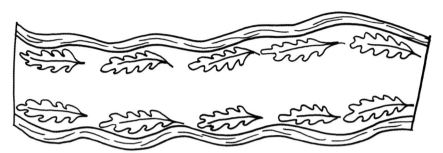

WAVY OAK LEAVES

Page 108

WAVY FLOWER POT

Page 109

MERMAIDS AT MIDNIGHT

Page 111

ROSY POSY POT

Page 112

About the Author

Deanne Fitzpatrick, of Amherst, Nova Scotia, is well known worldwide for her hooked rugs and patterns. Her work is in permanent exhibits at the Art Gallery of Nova Scotia and the Canadian Museum of Civilization, among others. Deanne is also the author of *Hook Me a Story: The History and Method of Rug Hooking in Atlantic Canada* (Nimbus, 1999). You can visit her online at www.hookingrugs.com.